W9-AEK-851

Bud E. Smith

Sams **Teach Yourself**

iPad™

in **10 Minutes**

SAMS | 800 East 96th Street, Indianapolis, Indiana 46240

International Standard Book Number-10: 0-672-33337-6

International Standard Book Number-13: 978-0-672-33337-8

Library of Congress Cataloging-in-Publication Data

Smith, Bud E.
  Sams teach yourself iPad in 10 minutes / Bud E. Smith.
    p. cm.
  Includes bibliographical references.
  ISBN 978-0-672-33337-8
  1. iPad (Computer) 2. Tablet computers. I. Title.
  QA76.8.I863S65 2011
  004.16—dc22

                                              2010025005

Printed in the United States of America
First Printing: July 2010

09 08 07 06   4 3 2 1

Trademarks

All terms mentioned in this book that are known to be trademarks or service marks have been appropriately capitalized. Pearson cannot attest to the accuracy of this information. Use of a term in this book should not be regarded as affecting the validity of any trademark or service mark.

Warning and Disclaimer

Every effort has been made to make this book as complete and as accurate as possible, but no warranty or fitness is implied. The information provided is on an "as is" basis. The author and the publisher shall have neither liability nor responsibility to any person or entity with respect to any loss or damages arising from the information contained in this book.

Bulk Sales

Pearson offers excellent discounts on this book when ordered in quantity for bulk purchases or special sales. For more information, please contact

> **U.S. Corporate and Government Sales**
> **1-800-382-3419**
> corpsales@pearsontechgroup.com

For sales outside of the U.S., please contact

> **International Sales**
> international@pearsoned.com

Associate Publisher
Greg Wiegand

Aquisitions Editor
Laura Norman

Development Editor
Lora Baughey

Technical Editor
Matthew David

Managing Editor
Sandra Schroeder

Project Editor
Mandie Frank

Copy Editor
Water Crest Publishing

Indexer
Cheryl Lenser

Production
Jake McFarland

Proofreader
Williams Woods Publishing

Book Designer
Gary Adair

Contents

About the Author

Bud Smith has written and edited many books over the last 25 years covering a wide variety of computer topics, including guides to buying a computer, using all kinds of software, and doing almost anything you can think of online. His most recent title is *Sams Teach Yourself Tumblr in 10 Minutes*, with in-depth coverage of the new, exciting micro-blogging platform.

Bud began writing computer books back in 1984, the year of the iconic 1984 television commercial for the Macintosh. An early success was his *Computer's Buyer's Guide for Que*, covering the then-latest and greatest in computer hardware and software. Bud continues to work as a writer, project manager, and marketer to help people get the most out of technology as it advances. He currently lives in the San Francisco Bay Area, participating in environmental causes when he's not working on one of his many technology-related projects.

Dedication

This book is dedicated to Mark Middlebrook, for being a friend indeed.

Acknowledgments

The first person to thank is Laura Norman, who brought me straight from co-authoring the *Sams Teach Yourself Tumblr in 10 Minutes* book to this exciting project; to development editor Lora Baughey, for helping bring one of the first mainstream books about iPad into being; to copy editor Sarah Kearns, for helping straighten snarled syntax; to technical editor Matthew David, for making sure everything said here is true and correct; and finally to the production team at Pearson, who applied their talents to bring my insights about using the iPad into the useful and attractive *Teach Yourself* format. Special thanks to Judith, for encouragement all along the way. Also, thanks to the many people who are making this very cool new tool their own.

We Want to Hear from You

As the reader of this book, you are our most important critic and commentator. We value your opinion and want to know what we're doing right, what we could do better, what areas you'd like to see us publish in, and any other words of wisdom you're willing to pass our way.

You can email or write me directly to let me know what you did or didn't like about this book—as well as what we can do to make our books stronger.

Please note that I cannot help you with technical problems related to the topic of this book, and that due to the high volume of mail I receive, I might not be able to reply to every message.

When you write, please be sure to include this book's title and author, as well as your name and contact information. I will carefully review your comments and share them with the author and editors who worked on the book.

E-mail: consumer@samspublishing.com

Mail: Greg Wiegand
          Associate Publisher
          Sams Publishing
          800 East 96th Street
          Indianapolis, IN 46240 USA

Introduction

The iPad is the biggest thing to hit computing in years. Drawing on the best of Apple's iPhone and iPod touch products, and Apple's Macintosh personal computers, while introducing a whole new way of seeing and interacting with information, it has grabbed the imagination of the world.

Getting the most out of the iPad requires an active imagination, curiosity, and willingness to try new things. That's because it's physically fixed— you can't add memory or other hardware to the insides—but so easily customizable by your choice of which apps to buy (where needed), download, and run out of more than 100,000 available.

Many of you will not only face the challenge of getting the most out of the iPad yourself, but will also need to prepare for others to ask you for help with their own iPad questions. This book arms you to meet your own needs and to help out others as well.

The iPad experience has six important components. The first is the iPad itself, which is almost an object of art at the same time that it's a compelling device.

The second is the software that animates it: iPhone OS. This operating software, originally developed for the iPhone, has scaled up well to the demands of the much larger iPad. It maintains its simplicity, while bringing multi-touch interaction to a whole new level.

The third is the apps that come with the iPad, plus the ones you add yourself. These allow for learning, fun, and creativity. The apps ecosystem is a welcome byproduct of the iPhone's growth, now with a whole new canvas for developers to paint on.

The fourth part is the accessories you buy with the iPad, or after purchase. Useful for protecting, powering, or otherwise enhancing your use of the iPad, accessories are an important part of your purchase (and, most likely, a big chunk of your total iPad-related expenditures).

The fifth part is content that you download for playback on iPad. Including movies, TV shows, music, books, and more, this content takes advantage of the iPad as a powerful and portable playback device. Along with accessories, content is likely to make up a big part of your iPad-related expenditures.

The final part is the interaction you have, through software, with the Internet and the Web. Many apps are portals into different kinds of information, presented in different ways to make it as interesting and useful as the developer can manage.

This book gives you the skills to conduct the orchestra of different elements that make up the iPad, to manage your own team of apps on the playing field of the iPad and iPhone OS, and to get the most out of the great resources available in the software itself and on the Internet.

About This Book

As part of the *Sams Teach Yourself in 10 Minutes* guides, this book aims to teach you the ins and outs of using the iPad without using up a lot of precious time. Divided into easy-to-follow lessons that you can tackle in about 10 minutes each, you learn the following iPad tasks and topics:

- ▶ How to choose the iPad that's right for you

- ▶ How to buy accessories for your iPad, now and in the future

- ▶ How to manage the settings for your iPad and apps

- ▶ Getting online via Wi-Fi and, for iPads that support it, 3G

- ▶ Using iTunes to buy and synchronize multimedia—music, videos, movies, and more—between the computer and the iPad

- ▶ Using Safari to access the Web, working around problems

- ▶ Using iPhone email and Gmail, with and without a live connection

- ▶ Managing personal information with the Calendar, Contacts, and Notes

- ▶ Using maps, including the live Street View in its full-screen glory

- ▶ Getting full-screen iPad apps, as well as iPhone-sized apps from the App Store

▶ Getting and working with photos, movies, TV shows, and video

▶ Using iBooks and the new iBooks Store, introduced first on iPad

▶ Getting and playing music on iPad

▶ Using the iWork apps for writing presentations and working with numbers

▶ Using the Dock, external keyboard, and other accessories

▶ Hooking up to external devices such as a presentation screen or TV

▶ Understanding how to use the iPad accessibly

After you finish these lessons, and the others in this book, you'll know all you need to know to take your iPad with you as far as you want to go.

Who This Book Is For

This book is aimed at new iPad users who want to get the most out of the device. This includes people with and without iPhone experience and experience with the Mac, so all backgrounds and levels of experience are supported.

By providing depth along with introductory information, this book also helps you help others. New technology depends on and spreads among networks of family members, friends, and co-workers just as much as it depends on the Internet and global positioning satellite (GPS) systems.

The iPad will take a long time to reach full adoption, and the picture will be muddied for customers by the introduction of new devices with some similar and some different functionality. By giving you a solid grasp of the iPad right from the beginning, the book will not only help you, but will give you the answers when others want help getting the most out of their own iPads.

Each lesson focuses on one specific topic, such as getting the settings right for your iPad or getting online via Wi-Fi or 3G. You can skip from one topic to another, read the book through from start to finish, or both. You can also hand it to a friend, family member, or colleague to answer a specific question.

What Do I Need to Use This Book?

All you need to use most of this book is access to any kind of iPad. For some functions, you also need at least part-time access to the Internet via Wi-Fi or 3G. And there is detailed coverage here of a few apps and add-ons that don't come with the iPad out of the box, including a few that cost money, such as the iWork productivity suite and accessories.

The idea is to help you get the most out of your purchase of an iPad, to know what else might be worth spending money on, and to help you maximize the use of the most important paid apps and accessories if you do buy them. That way, the entire iPad world opens up to you in a way that helps you best manage your time and your money.

Conventions Used in This Book

Whenever you need to push a particular button on the iPad, or touch a particular control in the iPhone OS or in an app, you'll find the label or name for that item bolded in the text, such as "click the **Home** button." In addition to the text and figures in this book, you'll also encounter some special boxes labeled Tip, Note, or Caution.

> TIP: Tips offer helpful shortcuts or easier ways to do something.

> NOTE: Notes are extra bits of information related to the text that might help you expand your knowledge or understanding.

> CAUTION: Cautions are warnings or other important information you need to know about consequences of using a feature or executing a task.

Screen Captures

The figures captured for this book come from the iPad and show the iPhone OS, apps, and screenshots from the Safari web browser. You may use different settings for the iPhone and apps, and you will probably use at least some—maybe many—different apps than those featured in this book. For any of these reasons, your screens may look somewhat different than those in the book.

The iPhone OS is regularly updated with minor changes or more major new versions, and you may use newer versions of apps, different apps, or even a different web browser. Also keep in mind that the developers of the iPad and the apps and web sites shown in this book are constantly working to improve their software, web sites, and the services offered on them.

New features are added regularly to the iPhone OS, apps, and web services, and old ones change or disappear. This means the screen contents change often, so your own screens may differ from the ones shown in this book. Don't be too alarmed, however. The basics, though they are tweaked in appearance from time to time, stay mostly the same in principle and usage.

LESSON 1

Introducing iPad

In this lesson, you learn about the iPad device—what's inside it, how to use its buttons and controls, and what you see onscreen when you first start it.

The iPad Inside and Out

"A thing of beauty is a joy forever," wrote John Keats, and the iPad is a beautiful thing. Its simple design and very small number of visible controls makes it seem useful and friendly.

To get the most out of it, you should understand the function of every button and control that it has, and something about the insides as well. What the iPad *doesn't* have, compared to a full personal computer, is just as important as what it *does* have.

iPad Size, Weight, and Specifications

The iPad is sized a lot like a pad of letter-size paper: about 10" tall and 7 1/2" wide, and only half an inch deep, as shown in Figure 1.1. It weighs just a pound and a half—half of a typical netbook's weight—and only a third or a quarter the weight of a typical notebook computer. (You'll still feel that pound and a half as being a bit heavy after more than a few minutes of, say, reading from the iPad in bed.)

The iPad's size and weight is directly relevant to how you'll use it. In terms of size, carrying the iPad is easier even than carrying around a paper notebook, and in terms of weight, the iPad is only a little heavier. You may not want to carry it in a way that's visible to others, because of the danger of loss or theft, but it slips into a large purse or a small carrying case easily.

FIGURE 1.1 The iPad is lovely and compact.

> **NOTE: A Margin for Error?**
> The screen display that you see when you turn on the device doesn't, unfortunately, fill the available space; it has a border of about three fourths of an inch all around. Perhaps a future version of the iPad will fill in that margin.

The iPad's screen is 9.7" diagonally, and has 1024 x 768 resolution in landscape mode. The 1024 x 768 resolution figure is an old computer spec—a typical widescreen laptop today is 1280 x 800, much wider, and about one-third larger in total resolution. The screen works equally well in landscape or portrait mode, and the iPad switches modes for you as you turn it; you can never turn it the wrong way, though you might occasionally have a hard time finding just where the Home button is.

The iPad's resolution is not quite that of a widescreen device, so some fully widescreen content is letterboxed, with blank strips of blackness above and below, to play on it. Other content is shown with full vertical resolution (height) and with a bit cut off on each end, which is not usually a problem.

The screen resolution is 132 pixels per inch, a bit denser than a typical computer screen. The screen is fingerprint-resistant and pretty much spillproof, but you'll want to be careful not to scratch it, and to have a good glasses cleaning cloth or cleaning kit to keep it as shiny as when it was new.

> **NOTE: Consider Protecting Your Screen**
> One accessory you may want to consider is a screen protector film for your iPad. It protects the screen and doesn't seem to detract from the touch sensitivity or brightness much. If you're uncertain, consider visiting a shop to see if you can try an iPad with the screen protector applied.

iPad Buttons and Controls

The iPad has only eight buttons, controls, connectors, and input/output ports. Look closely at your iPad to see them—three on the top edge, one at the bottom of the screen, two on the right edge, and two on the bottom edge. Here's a brief description of each, and what it does for you:

▶ **Home button** (bottom center of screen, in portrait mode). The Home button always takes you back to the Home screen. As on the iPhone, the Home button is an important key to the iPad's simplicity and usefulness.

▶ **Sleep/Wake button** (top-right edge). The iPad has no moving parts, so there's nothing to start or stop. If you press it briefly, the Sleep/Wake button instantly takes the iPad from an almost no-power mode, with the screen completely off, to powered up. If you press it for longer, the Sleep/Wake button turns the iPad on and off.

▶ **Microphone** (top-left edge). A tiny hole, as on many phones.

▶ **Headphone jack** (top-left edge). A larger hole for a 3.5mm headphone jack. Many headphones you might have lying around will fit this.

▶ **Screen rotation block** (top-right edge). A switch that keeps the screen from re-orienting when you turn the iPad around. Great for avoiding vertigo from the screen spinning about when you're reading in bed or laying the iPad flat on a desk.

▶ **Volume up/down** (top-right edge). A rocker switch that does what it says on the tin. Press the top part (near the corner of the iPad's edges) to turn up the volume, press the lower part (away from the corner) to turn down the volume.

▶ **Speaker** (bottom-right edge). A small grill on the lower-right edge of the iPad with three openings, it gives surprisingly good sound.

▶ **Dock connector** (bottom edge, center).

The dock connector can provide a multitude of functions. Any device that connects to it must be made by, or approved by, Apple, which is good for your peace of mind (in terms of quality) and their profits (they charge a licensing fee for others).

The iPad lacks many typical computer connectors, but most visibly and consequentially, it lacks any USB connectors—not even one. This is a huge source of frustration to the computer-oriented press, and also to many users who have invested a lot in various USB-connected devices, such as a mouse (for a humble example) or a printer (there's no printing from the iPad!). However, Apple's tight control of peripherals does contribute to the overall high quality of the iPad and its ecosystem of hardware and software.

Using iPad Controls

Using the iPad controls is simple. You can lock it, turn it on or off, and even capture a screen image.

The iPad has a sleep state and a fully off state. In the sleep state, it powers (partway) down very quickly, uses very little power, and comes back on very quickly. (Going to sleep and waking each take less than a second.)

In the fully off state, the iPad uses no power at all, though the battery might discharge very gradually, over many months.

When the iPad first comes back on, whether from sleep or being off, it goes into a locked mode (see Figure 1.2). That means the iPad is

FIGURE 1.2   The iPad needs your help to fully awaken.

insensitive to any input except your finger bringing a slider across a gap of about 2" from left to right. If you don't unlock the screen fairly quickly—within about 5 seconds—the device goes back to sleep. This is to prevent accidentally turning on the device into full-power mode, and is also where you'll see the password entry screen if you choose to use password protection as well. (See Lesson 3, "Editing Text and Using Multi-Touch," for the relevant settings.)

Table 1.1 shows how to use the iPad's controls to manage the iPad.

TABLE 1.1   Using the iPad's Controls to Get Things Done

Task	Steps
Turn iPad off	Hold down the Power button for about three seconds, which brings up a red slider at the top of the screen. Slide the slider across the screen to complete turning the iPad fully off.
Put iPad to sleep	Press and release the Power button, but do not hold it down.
Turn iPad on after sleep	Hold down the Power button briefly, which brings up a green slider at the bottom of the screen. Slide the slider across the screen to complete turning the iPad fully on.
Turn iPad on after power-off	Hold down the Power button briefly, but longer than for turning on the iPad after sleep—about a full second. (A brief touch, when the iPad is fully off, has no effect.) The Apple icon will display for about ten seconds, and then a green slider appears at the bottom of the screen. Slide the slider across the screen to complete turning the iPad fully on.
Stop screen image from rotating	Get the iPad screen in the desired orientation; then slide the screen rotation lock down.
Allow screen image to rotate	Slide the screen rotation lock up.
Change volume	Press the Volume Up or Volume Down button. Mute is achieved by continuing to hold the Power Down button until the volume is zero.
Return to Home screen	Press the Home button.

TABLE 1.1 Continued

Task	Steps
Take a screenshot	To capture the current screen image, press the On/Off button and then quickly press the Home button. There will be a white flash and a click, and the current screen image will be saved into the Photo application.

Inside the iPad

The most important thing about the inside of the iPad is that you're never supposed to need to see it. The iPad is not user-openable or upgradable; if you try to open it, you not only void the warranty, you risk breaking the device so it won't close up again—an unnecessary waste of a few hundred dollars.

The inside of the iPad contains several elements worthy of note, as follows:

- ▶ **A4 processor.** The A4 central processing unit inside the iPad runs at up to 1GHz, which is very fast indeed compared to most smartphones, but slower than a personal computer. The A4 processor controls graphics as well as standard computer processing, and is thought to be carefully engineered for power management and cool operation.

- ▶ **16GB, 32GB, or 64GB of flash memory.** Instead of a hard disk, Apple provides storage as solid-state memory with no moving parts. The amount of RAM most directly affects how much music and video you can store on the device, as well as the price (about $100 for each step up in RAM size).

- ▶ **Wi-Fi and, optionally, 3G hardware.** All iPads have Wi-Fi built-in, but only some have 3G for cellular network access, and then only at a price (about $130 extra at launch).

▶ **Two big batteries.** Two long, tall, thin batteries totaling 25 watt-hours occupy almost all of the height and width, and about half the depth, of the iPad.

The system performance of these components has amazed even hardened computer and smartphone reviewers, who approvingly note that the iPad lasts even longer than the ten hours that Apple claims it does for just about any normal operations, such as watching video, using apps, surfing the Web, and so on.

iPad Accessories

The iPad has many different kinds of accessories. It's good to know the main classes of accessories in order to be able to know just how you can extend the usefulness of your iPad.

There are three types of accessories I'll mention here: accessories included with the iPad, Apple-offered accessories, and third-party accessories.

Accessories Included with the iPad

The iPad includes a 10W USB power adapter and a dock connector to USB cable. The 10W USB power adapter plugs into a socket. The cable plugs into the socket (on the USB end) and the iPad (on the dock connector end). This powers the device. The iPad takes several hours to recharge.

You can also recharge the iPad by plugging the USB end of the power adapter into a computer USB socket. However, this takes about twice as long—and "about" is very approximate, as USB power capabilities vary greatly, sometimes being different between two USB connectors on the same machine. It's better to think of this as an emergency measure than as a standard way to charge your iPad.

The iPad-to-computer USB connection is also vital, of course, for transferring data—music, movies, and more. Check to see how quickly your iPad recharges when plugged in for this purpose, so you know what to expect if you want or need to do it this way

You'll probably want more accessories. For instance, protecting the iPad's lovely finish and its screen have to be priorities. On the other hand, Steve Jobs once said that the scratches and dings on his iPhone were a form of weathering that made the device more attractive, not less, so everyone's needs are different. That's why most accessories are optional—and why picking them out is so much fun.

Accessories Available from Apple

Apple offers a number of accessories with the iPad—some of which are "must-haves," some of which should be considered along with third-party alternatives, and others of which are specialist tools.

Here's a brief rundown of the major types of accessories that Apple has an entry for, and a description of Apple's product, or products, in each. For alternatives, check online (Apple's site is Apple-only), in a physical Apple store (with both Apple and third-party products), and in other stores that carry electronic products (often including third-party products, but few Apple products).

iPad Case

Apple has designed a clever neoprene case for your iPad, shown (along with the keyboard dock) in Figure 1.3. Not only does it protect the device well, but when you fold it backward and tuck the edge of one side of the case into a flap on the back of the other side, it holds the iPad in landscape mode at an angle of about 20 degrees, like an old-fashioned lap desk. This is very useful for taking notes while sitting at a desk, whether you use the iPad onscreen keyboard or an external keyboard. It's not as good for watching videos, because you'd probably want the iPad up on a desk or table, and in a more steeply angled position.

There are bound to be many other cases for iPad, and some may be different in ways that make them a better fit for you, or better for use in some situations. However, at a price of $29, many will consider Apple's iPad case to be pretty much a must-have.

FIGURE 1.3   The iPad keyboard dock and case.

Docks and Keyboards

You will almost certainly want a dock for your iPad. The dock is a charging stand that holds up the iPad at a slight angle, so you can use it fairly easily while charging it, or keeping it charged.

There are two docks available from Apple: one integrates a keyboard with the dock, and the other is the dock by itself. Both docks have a plug for the dock connector to USB cable that comes with the iPad and an audio line-out port to connect speakers to sound coming from your iPad. (The audio cable you need for this is sold separately.)

The prices, at this writing, are $69 for the keyboard + dock combination unit, $29 for the standalone dock, and $69 for the standalone keyboard. So, the standalone dock plus keyboard costs $98, or $29 more than the keyboard + dock combination unit.

If you get the dock without a keyboard, you then have the option of buying Apple's wireless keyboard. It's a slender, single piece of aluminum, with a rolled edge at the top that holds the batteries and gives it a bit of altitude. The standalone dock and wireless keyboard are shown in Figure 1.4.

FIGURE 1.4 The simpler iPad dock and keyboard, and more.

I prefer the simpler dock and the standalone keyboard for flexibility. With the standalone keyboard, you can sit back in a chair typing at your iPad a few feet away, and can carry around the keyboard and the iPad, without needing the dock, to go mobile.

People swear by them, but having a keyboard, no matter how gorgeous, with your iPad is a bit odd. The keyboard does make entering text much easier, but it takes your hands away from the iPad's touchscreen. There's no mouse, so to move the cursor around onscreen, you have to touch the screen. Selecting is quite tricky, and you may find yourself setting down the keyboard, taking the iPad out of the dock, selecting text, and then returning everything back to normal.

The bottom line is that the keyboard, in either form, is quite useful sometimes, but it doesn't make an iPad into a full personal computer—they're still quite different.

Power and Connector Cables

Apple sells power and connector cables for the iPad, as follows:

▶ **10W USB Power Adapter with 6' cord.** A suitable replacement for, or addition to, the 10W USB Power Adapter with a too-short 3' cord that Apple includes with the iPad. If you buy the new one, you can use the old one as a travel kit. Price: $29.

▶ **Camera Connection Kit.** Lets you send photos directly from a camera's USB port or directly from an SD card, without using a computer as an intermediary. Great if you take many pictures, and it lets you use the iPad and its Wi-Fi and/or 3G wireless connection to transmit photos to others on the go. Price: $29.

▶ **iPad Dock Connector to VGA Adapter.** VGA input to a monitor, TV, and so on. Price: $29.

▶ **Apple Composite AV Cable and Apple Component AV Cable.** If you want to send both streaming video and full stereo sound to a big-screen TV, you need one of these cables or the other, depending on which works with your big-screen TV. Price: $49 for either.

CAUTION: **Check Electrical Licenses**

Don't use unlicensed electronics products with your iPad, due to the potential electrical and fire dangers of anything electronic that doesn't meet all applicable standards.

These power and connector cables are all perfectly adequate. However, any time you see a bunch of different things priced the same, you suspect that at least some of them might actually be available for less. You may want to shop around to check out competitors for some of these products, to the extent that Apple allows them to exist by granting licenses for them.

Earphones and Headphones

Earphones and headphones are very much an item of personal taste—and that is likely to require a personal trial as well. Unless you're in a big hurry to get this part of your iPad-related shopping over with, consider going to an Apple store or other store and trying out some different headphones before committing.

Apple offers two different kinds of earphones for the iPad, shown previously in Figure 1.4:

- ▶ **Earphones with Remote and Mic.** This is a very phone-like pair of earphones with a remote control and microphone on the cable. The use for the microphone is a bit obscure, as there's no approved way to make phone calls or video calls on your iPad, but the price is low enough that you can buy this just for the non-microphone bits. Price: $29.

- ▶ **In-Ear Headphones with Remote and Mic.** The name In-Ear Headphones is meant to imply higher quality than plain old earphones. Experts say that you can get a lot more enjoyment from music by upgrading your earphones or headphones just a little bit, and this is Apple's bid to sell you the recommended upgrade.

Apple has put together a couple of credible offerings here by having two products originally created for the iPhone, which does, of course, support phone calls. This is the one item, however, that you're almost sure to want to shop for in person, and try competing products at various price levels, before deciding.

There are very inexpensive and very fancy earphones, noise-canceling headphones, clever on-ear and around-ear headphones, and much more. It's worth checking out these products in person before buying.

Third-Party Accessories

The iPod music player and the iPhone have incited a tidal wave of accessories, and the iPad is no different. Here are some of the major categories of accessories to consider if you are ready to go shopping, online or in person:

- ▶ **Adapters and chargers.** Power adapters like the ones Apple offers, plus adapters for cars and many others as well.

▸ **Batteries.** The iPad's 10-hour charge reduces the need for an add-on battery, but there will always be people who need more. Add-on batteries plug in to keep your iPad going when it's otherwise out of power, but of course they add weight and bulk.

▸ **Cases and skins.** Every material, thickness, color, and degree of protection you can imagine has been, or probably will be, made for the iPad.

▸ **Cables.** Longer and different kinds of charging and data transfer cables.

▸ **Earphones and headsets.** Every taste accounted for.

▸ **Keyboards.** Foldable, slimmer, and less-expensive alternatives to Apple's aluminum marvel.

▸ **Screen protectors.** Many different screen protective films, pre-cut to fit the iPad.

▸ **Speakers.** You can make your own home stereo system based around your iPad.

▸ **Stylus pens.** Use a special stylus instead of a finger for more accurate and quicker data entry.

The possibilities, within these categories and in addition to them, are almost endless. For instance, if your iPad is feeding your TV or stereo, can a remote control for it be far behind? Use your imagination to come up with a new idea today, and you'll probably see it in the iPad store tomorrow.

Summary

In this lesson, you learned about the iPad's specifications and what they mean for using it, the iPad's hardware controls and how to use them, what's inside the iPad, and the Apple accessories available for it. In the next lesson, you'll find out how to set up and work with the iPad's Home screen features.

LESSON 2

Setting Up and Using the Home Screen

In this lesson, you learn your way around the iPad screen—what's on it, what all the little symbols in the Status bar and changes in them mean, and how to customize the app layout onscreen. You also learn how to search data you've entered across your iPad's apps.

The iPad's Touchscreen

Apple had a huge success with the Macintosh many years ago, largely as the result of the Mac's fully integrated use of a relatively new invention: the computer mouse. On the Mac, the mouse was used to do amazing things, such as driving the interface to professional-level drawing applications on an affordable personal computer.

Apple then recognized touch as the next big thing in computer interfaces, and started working to embrace and extend its use. The first big step was the integration of multi-touch capabilities as the main interaction tool for iPod music players and the iPhone. This technology has also been integrated into the trackpads for Mac portables, where multi-finger gestures control a variety of user interaction.

The iPad is the next logical evolution in the use of touch, and it represents a giant step forward. Being able to view personal computer-type content and tools and interact with them on a nearly full-size computer screen, but with full portability, is instantly understood by nearly everyone who tries using an iPad as a breakthrough.

The iPad screen is a rich, responsive, and wonderful thing, engineered, in hardware and software, to be as touch-friendly as any computing device ever made. To get the most out of it, you should understand some of the details of the way it works.

Status Icons

The status bar is the main mode for communication about the state of your iPad. It's like a bulletin board for messages from the iPad to you. Being able to quickly scan and understand what you do—and don't—see in the status bar as you use your iPad will help you get a lot more out of it.

There are several different types of status icons. Details for the settings that help you control each type of icon are given in later lessons. Following are the icons themselves and what they mean to you.

Wireless Communications Icons

Bluetooth is a protocol for transferring data between devices near each other. You should turn on Bluetooth when needed, such as when you're about to use a wireless keyboard. You should turn off Bluetooth at other times, as it uses power, and can be used to try to steal information off your computer when you're out and about.

To turn Bluetooth on or off, press Settings>General, then press Bluetooth, and use the slider to toggle it on or off.

There are four possible ways for your iPad to transfer data over the Internet—Wi-Fi (available on all iPads), and three progressively faster and more capable types of data transfer over a cellphone wireless network: GPRS (also known as 2G), EDGE (also known as 2.5G), and 3G. These types of data transfer are only available on iPad Wi-Fi+3G models.

Also only available on iPad Wi-Fi+3G models is Airplane mode, which turns off all Internet access and Bluetooth.

The activity icon displays network activity, such as refreshing a web page, and some other activity as well. It's used as an indicator by third-party applications to show they're working.

The VPN icon shows if you're connected to a virtual private network. This is usually only applicable if you have the okay to use your iPad for work or school and are accessing your organization's servers via your iPad.

To sum up, at any given time, you'll see up to four icons for wireless communication on a Wi-Fi-only iPad, and the following icons showing for wireless communication:

> ▶ **Bluetooth**, if Bluetooth is available for connections. (Turn off Bluetooth when you aren't specifically using it.)

> ▶ **Wi-Fi**, if you're connected to a Wi-Fi network.

> ▶ **VPN**, if you're connected to a virtual private network.

> ▶ **Activity**, for network and some other kinds of activity.

> ▶ iPad Wi-Fi+3G only: **GPRS, EDGE, 3G**, or **Airplane** mode, if you either are connected to a cellphone wireless network (GPRS, EDGE, and 3G) or have turned off wireless access (Airplane mode).

In Airplane mode, Bluetooth, Wi-Fi, and cellphone wireless are shut off. If you're on an airplane with a Wi-Fi-only iPad, just turn off Bluetooth and Wi-Fi.

Other Icons

Most of the possible icons in the Status bar relate to wireless communication. There are only four others:

> ▶ **Battery.** Shows the current battery charging level and charging status. (The words "not charging" are displayed when not connected to power, or when connected to a USB port that doesn't power the iPad.)

> ▶ **Play.** A song, audiobook, or podcast is playing. See Lesson 15, "Using iBooks and the iBook Store," for details.

> ▶ **Lock.** Shows that the screen is locked. You'll already know this because the iPad will be displaying the unlock screen.

> ▶ **Screen rotation lock.** Shows that the screen rotation lock is on.

Included Apps

If apps are the secret of getting the most out of the iPad, the included apps are "the secret of the secret." New, exciting apps that become available through the App Store seem to get all the attention, whether free or downloaded. Yet many people don't spend enough time using the included apps to full advantage, repeatedly chasing new apps, when the ones that everyone already has can get an awful lot of the things you need done.

Dock Apps

There are four apps in the Dock, the bottom bar of the iPad Home screen. Not only is the Dock available on the first pane of the Home screen; it's available on every pane.

These key apps are as follows:

> ▶ **Safari.** This is the built-in web browser for the iPad, and the portal to a great deal of functionality, whenever you have Internet access via Wi-Fi or the cellphone wireless network. If you use a different browser—at this writing, the Opera browser is available for iPhone and iPad—then you may want to put that in the bottom browser bar instead.

> ▶ **Mail.** Apple's built-in mail. See Lesson 7, "Synching, Sending, and Receiving Email," for details.

> ▶ **Photos.** The Photos app is only used for viewing photos, because the iPad doesn't take photos. You can use the Camera Connection Kit to attach a camera directly to your iPad and download photos via the Web or PC to build up your stock on iPad.

> ▶ **iPod.** The iPod app is the interface to music on your iPad. The iPad is a fantastic music machine, and the iPad's somewhat limited multitasking has strong support for playing music in the background. If you use a streaming app, or some other app for music instead of iPad, consider putting that other app on the bottom bar instead.

The bottom bar can actually accommodate up to six apps. Consider replacing and adding to the original four apps in the bottom bar to create a working set of the apps you use the most, and that you want available on every pane of the Home screen. Customizing the Home screen is explained later in this lesson.

> TIP: **Status and Dock Always Visible**
>
> The Status bar at the top and the Dock of selected app icons at the bottom are always visible on all Home screens.

Home Screen Apps

The home screen includes nine additional apps, and you may want to consider adding the iBooks app to this core group as well, to make a total of ten. Here are brief descriptions of all of them:

▶ **Calendar.** The Calendar app trades information with other calendars: Apple's iCal and MobileMe, Microsoft Entourage (Mac) and Microsoft Outlook (Windows) personal information managers, and Microsoft Exchange, commonly used by medium-sized and large organizations. (Yahoo! Calendar and Google Calendar are notable exceptions here.)

▶ **Contacts.** Syncs with Apple's MobileMe and MacOS X Address Book; Yahoo! Address Book and Google Contacts; Microsoft Outlook, Microsoft Exchange, and Windows Address Book as used by Microsoft Express.

▶ **Notes.** The Notes app is highly underrated (I've even heard people complain about the font it uses). It's a free, easy-to-use tool that replaces a paper notepad, and is easier to carry than a paper notepad (and with far more flexibility). It's also much easier to carry than a laptop, and much less obtrusive in use. It just takes one button push to send your (scrolling) page of notes out as an email message, which is highly convenient for sending out notes just after a meeting. See Lesson 8, "Using Contacts and Notes," for details.

▶ **Maps.** The Maps app, from Google, is great—it even supports Street View in glorious full-screen. However, Maps lacks turn-by-turn directions, which are found for free on some Google Android devices, and is frustrating to use with a Wi-Fi-only iPad rather than an iPad Wi-Fi+3G. Lesson 10, "Working with Maps," has more information.

▶ **Videos.** Plays video content—including movies, TV shows, video podcasts, and other videos you buy on iTunes or play from your own collection. See Lesson 13, "Playing Videos and YouTube," for details on videos and YouTube as well.

▶ **YouTube.** Does what it says on the tin—a direct, full-screen interface into YouTube and its collection of videos. You can search or browse categories and do everything a YouTube account will allow, such as add ratings to videos, synchronize favorites between your iPad and personal computer, and more.

▶ **iTunes.** Direct access to the iTunes store, which you can search for all kinds of media, including music, audiobooks, music videos, TV shows, movies, and more. You can then download what you need directly to your iPad. As on YouTube, you can review items (see Lesson 5, "Customizing General Settings for Your iPad").

▶ **App Store.** The famous Apple App Store contains a mix of apps totalling more than a hundred thousand, though most are not yet iPad-optimized. Shopping for an app, when you don't already know which one you want by name, can be difficult—there are more than 100,000 apps in the App Store, and they are not all that well-organized—but fun. Lesson 10 and Lesson 11, "Getting Apps from the App Store," have details.

▶ **Settings.** iPad has surprisingly simple core settings for all it does, while apps have their own settings in this area as well. Settings are covered in Lesson 4, "Getting Connected to Wi-Fi, 3G, and Bluetooth."

▶ **iBook.** iBook is Apple's online bookstore and includes hundreds of thousands of titles, free and paid. The app doesn't currently show up on the Home screen because it wasn't available from Apple at launch, but you should add it to other core Apple apps (no pun intended), as described later in this lesson, as soon as you're ready to check it out. Lesson 15, "Using iBooks and the iBookstore," has details.

One key decision to make going in is whether you're going to use the iPad for personal information management, such as your contacts and the calendar. The iPad is a really cool way to do this, but if you already handle it through your personal computer and/or smartphone, you may not want to do it on the iPad as well.

If your smartphone is an iPhone, personal information management may more or less automatically get handled on the iPad as well. Otherwise, think carefully about whether you want to handle these updates on the iPad instead of, or in addition to, a smartphone, or just not bother with that on the iPad.

If you have an iPad Wi-Fi+3G that you tend to carry around with you almost, or fully, as much as a smartphone, it might make sense. However, your iPad is not where you handle phone calls or text messages from, so a key interactive function of personal information management is missing. Also, the iPad is easier to type on than an iPhone, but not as easy as a laptop. You may not want the hassle of using personal information management apps on the iPad.

Using the Home Screen

The iPad's Home screen has several panes, areas for additional icons that you reach by swiping onscreen to move left or right among the panes. The panes are home to icons for various apps—the original set that comes with your iPad, plus additional apps you've downloaded and installed.

An app bar appears across the bottom of the screen, and remains in place even when you change panes. When you get your iPad, the app bar includes the built-in Safari Web browser and the Mail, Photos, and iPod apps. However, you can change which apps are in the app bar, and add up to two more apps to it for a total of six.

The Home screen also includes the following:

▶ **A Search screen.** This screen appears to the left of the core Home screen. To reach it, press the Home button; then drag your finger horizontally, left to right, to scroll by one screen.

▶ **The core Home screen.** The core Home screen is where you return when you press the Home button. This screen should have your most-used app icons, for speed of starting frequently used apps.

▶ **Additional Home screens.** As you add and move app icons to the Home screen, additional Home screens are added—or, when necessary, removed—to the right of the core Home screen. To reach them, press the Home button to return to the core Home screen, and then scroll to the right to reach the additional Home screens.

The overall Home screen expands with additional screens to fit the apps you put on it, up to a total of 11 screens with up to 20 apps each, or up to 220 apps total. (You can also put apps in folders, allowing you to have many more.)

The term "Home screen" refers to all the screens together and also to the one, single, original Home screen, which includes a Search screen to its left and that never goes away, even if you throw away all your apps.

You can think of it as being like a folding room divider with up to 11 screens, plus a search screen to the left of the first, original Home screen. Dots on every screen of the overall Home screen show how many separate screens there are, and the lit dot shows which one you're on. See Figure 2.1 for an example.

Using the Home screen is easy, as follows:

▶ **Returning to the core Home screen.** To return to the core Home screen from any other iPad screen, press the Home button.

▶ **Scrolling among the Home screens.** To scroll among the Home screens, just swipe horizontally from one screen to the next. Or, press to the left of the row of dots to scroll one screen left; press to the right of the row of dots to scroll one screen right. To continue scrolling by an additional screen, press again.

FIGURE 2.1   The Home screen includes dots that show you where you are.

▶ **Reaching the Search screen.** To reach the Search screen, press
   the Home button to return to the core Home screen; then scroll
   one screen to the left.

Customizing the Home Screen

Customizing the Home screen for the iPad is easy. Doing so makes your
iPad work the way you want it to, making it faster and simpler to get
things done.

Here's what you do to customize your Home screen:

▶ **To move an app on the same screen.** Press and hold an app icon
   until all the app icons start shaking, and an X appears in the
   upper left of each icon, as shown in Figure 2.2. Drag the app to
   any spot on the screen—whether empty or occupied. The app
   icon will relocate to the spot you drag it to or, if you've dragged

it into empty space beyond the other apps, it will relocate to the first empty position.

FIGURE 2.2   Pressing one app makes them all shake.

▶ **To remove an app icon, delete the app and its data.** After you've pressed an app icon and started them all quivering, press the X on the upper left corner of any app you want to remove. The app icon, the app code, and any documents and data created by the application are deleted, and can't be recovered.

▶ **To update the Dock.** You can move app icons to the Dock (up to six icons), remove app icons from the Dock onto any Home screen, and remove app icons completely that are resident on the Dock. No matter what Home screen you're on when you update the Dock, after you make changes to the Dock app icons, the updated Dock appears the same on all screens.

▶ **To move an app to a new screen.** Once the app icons are shaking, drag an app icon to the left or right edge of the screen. Hold it at the very edge, in a narrow region bordering the current screen and the screen off to the side. (This takes a bit of practice to get good at.) The screen will change from the previous location of the icon to the new screen you targeted.

▶ **To add a screen (up to 11 screens total).** If all screens are full, installing a new app (see Lesson 11) creates a new screen, with the new app's icon on it. Also, you can add a screen by dragging an app icon beyond the right edge of the current rightmost screen. You can add apps or keep dragging an icon to the right, creating new screens, for up to a total of 11 screens.

▶ **To use apps after changes.** After you've made desired changes, press the Home screen button once. The app icons will stop shaking, the X on each icon will disappear, and the number of dots shown to reflect the number of screens in the overall Home screen will update to reflect current usage.

Now you know how to customize your Home screen—but how do you want it to work? You can group app icons into sensible groups. That way, instead of finding one app icon out of as many as 220 on up to 11 screens, you first find the group of icons you want and then the specific app icon. This can be much easier, if the groups make sense.

TIP: **Try Moving Apps**

Experiment with moving apps around and creating new screens when you have a few spare minutes. That way, when you need to do it later on, it will be easy.

Think of your apps as being in groups: tools, news, games, and so on. Arrange the icons into sensible groups, a row, half-screen, or full screen at a time, by theme.

There's no way to label a screen or area with a name, so the groups have to be clear and self-evident. You can put an iconic app in the upper-left corner of a group to help, such as putting a BBC News app in the upper-left corner of a group of news apps. Just having the word "News" in the app icon name "BBC News" will remind you what the group is about.

Searching iPad

You can search the entire iPad from the Home screen using a screen called Spotlight. Spotlight searches the data you've entered into apps, including the Notes app, Mail, Calendar, Contacts, iPod, and Video.

Here's what Spotlight searches:

- ▶ **Applications.** Names of all apps, whether built in or installed.

- ▶ **Notes.** Names of notes and note text.

- ▶ **Mail.** To, From, and Subject fields (but not the content of email messages) across all accounts.

- ▶ **Calendar.** Event titles, names of people invited, and locations.

- ▶ **Contacts.** First names, last names, and company names.

- ▶ **iPod.** Names or titles of songs, podcasts, and audiobooks, as well as artists and albums for songs.

- ▶ **Video.** Names of videos.

You can use Settings to change which apps are searched, and even the order in which they're searched (see Lesson 5).

With many apps, you can also search within individual apps by using Spotlight from within the app. (The developer has to implement support for Spotlight searching in the app to make it available to you. Having Spotlight search support doesn't make sense for all apps, such as many games.)

NOTE: **Don't Worry About iPad Files**

Unlike a personal computer, the iPad does not have a user-accessible file system. That is, you can't get at all the files that iPhone OS, or a given app, might have. Instead, files are controlled by specific apps, which may give you access to files in different ways, or may not give you access to some or all files.

The whole idea of a "file" is more or less kept hidden from you. For instance, the notepad in the Notes app has many different pages in it, which you can access from a scrolling list on the left (see Lesson 8). You don't ever know whether the Notes app keeps these pages as separate files, or as separate parts of a single file. Part of the purpose of Spotlight is to help you get at your data, across platforms, without exposing (or making you understand and use) the file system.

To search the iPad, follow these steps:

1. Scroll horizontally to the Search screen, on the far left of the Home screen.

2. Use the onscreen keyboard to enter the search term you want to use.

3. Press the Search button on the keypad.

A list of search hits in various applications appears, as shown in Figure 2.3.

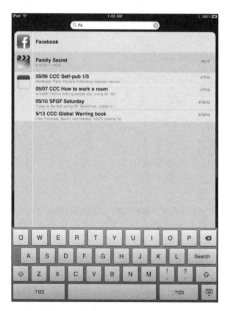

FIGURE 2.3 Searching from the Home screen gives you answers across apps.

To search within an app, open the app and then repeat the preceding steps. The results will reflect the contents of data entered into that app only.

Changing the Brightness and Wallpaper Settings

The Brightness and Wallpaper controls are grouped together on your
Settings menu, as they both affect the way your iPad screen looks as
you're using it. The controls are shown in Figure 2.4.

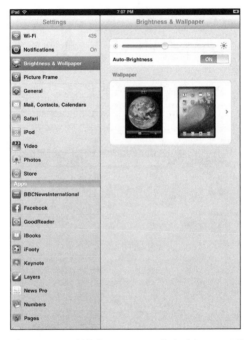

FIGURE 2.4   Brightness and Wallpaper controls help you get the look of
your iPad right.

Changing Brightness Settings

The brightness of your iPad screen affects not only the way your iPad
looks, but the way all your apps look. Here are some of the tradeoffs for
brightness:

▶ More brightness makes the screen look great, especially photos.
   It also seems easier to read or look at, at first.

▶ More brightness tires your eyes quicker. Some people have compared reading from the iPad to staring into a light bulb.

▶ Lower brightness is better for battery life. The screen is the single biggest power user on the iPad. The battery life of the iPad is so long (rated at roughly 10 hours of continuous use) that this may not be a big concern for you, but if you find yourself running out of battery power when using your iPad, reducing the brightness level should make a big difference.

▶ Lower brightness is better for sustained reading. This is why the iBooks app, described in Lesson 15, has its own brightness control.

You're likely to do a lot of reading in other apps such as the Safari Web browser, so brightness is important no matter what you're doing with your iPad.

Follow these steps to change the screen brightness of your iPad:

1. From the Home screen, tap Settings.

2. From the Settings screen, tap Brightness and Wallpaper. The Brightness & Wallpaper settings appear.

3. To change the brightness level, drag the slider left (dimmer) or right (brighter). The screen instantly gets brighter or dimmer in response.

4. Use the slider to turn the Auto-Brightness feature on or off.

If Auto-Brightness is on, the screen will adjust, using the built-in ambient (or "surrounding") light sensor. The screen automatically dims in low light, so as to not tire your eyes, and brightens in bright light, so as to compete with the bright surroundings.

Changing Wallpaper Settings

Wallpaper is simply the background image on your iPad screen. The image that ships on the iPad before you change it is a time exposure of a meteor shower, showing the meteors as streaks across the sky. Unfortunately, the streaks can look all too much like scratches in your iPad screen!

Luckily, it's easy and fun to change your wallpaper settings, choosing from the roughly 20 built-in images or any photo that you have on your iPad.

There are actually two different wallpaper choices you can make:

▶ Lock screen. This is the screen you see when your iPad has been locked and you use the slider that appears to unlock it.

▶ Home screen. This is the background for the several panes of your Home screen.

You can easily choose to use the same wallpaper on both for consistency.

Follow these steps to change the wallpaper for your iPad:

1. From the Home screen, tap Settings.

2. From the Settings screen, tap Brightness and Wallpaper. The Brightness & Wallpaper settings appear, including miniature versions of the current lock screen and home screen wallpaper.

3. To change the wallpaper for the lock screen, the home screen, or both, tap Wallpaper. You're given a choice of folders to choose from: A Wallpaper folder of built-in photos, plus multiple folders representing all the photos on your iPad.

4. Tap the folder you want to look in. A group of photos appears.

5. Tap the photo you want to inspect. The photo appears onscreen, along with buttons to use in setting the wallpaper for the two screens, as shown in Figure 2.5.

6. Tap the button, Set Lock Screen, to set the current photo as the lock screen photo; tap the button, Set Home Screen, to set the current photo as the home screen photo; tap Set Both to use the current photo for both.

7. Tap Back to return to the list of folders and make further choices or Home to return to the home screen.

FIGURE 2.5   Choose a great photo or two for your wallpaper.

> TIP: **Get Your Choice of Image Onscreen**
> You can use any image on your iPad for the lock screen and/or the home screen wallpaper. See Lesson 12, "Importing and Viewing Photos," for details on importing photos.

Summary

In this lesson, you learned about the iPad's Home screen and its contents, including status bar notification icons and the Dock of app icons at the bottom. You also learned how to change the apps arrangement and how to search for data across iPad's apps. In the next lesson, you will learn about entering and editing text using the iPad's on-screen keyboard among other options, as well as how to use the features of the multi-touch screen.

LESSON 3

Editing Text and Using Multi-Touch

In this lesson, you learn how to enter text using the iPad screen, including the onscreen keyboard and the Dictionary, and how to use multi-touch on the iPad—the biggest multi-touch-enabled surface from Apple yet.

Entering and Editing Text

The iPad is a breakthrough in many ways. Perhaps the single most important breakthrough is that it's the most ambitious attempt yet to offer computer-like functionality without a physical keyboard.

There is a whole raft of devices of all sizes that do have physical keyboards, including laptop computers, netbooks, and the BlackBerry line of smartphones. Apple has been a real pioneer of keyboard-less devices, with the iPhone, iPod Touch, and now the iPad.

Even more than the iPhone, the iPad and its apps are set up to reduce information entry. The device is heavily slanted toward the consumption, rather than the creation, of information. The iPad system software and apps are designed to gather data from wherever they can and reduce user input to a minimum. The challenge of entering information onto the iPad is met in three ways, as follows:

- ▶ **Offering choices rather than typed-in information.** The iPad and its apps tend to offer options and choices rather than requiring information to be typed in.

- ▶ **Offering onscreen keyboard(s).** The iPad offers system support for an onscreen keyboard, with options. The keyboard changes as you use it to offer portrait-mode and landscape-mode versions, different button choices for Web vs. other use, and so on. For instance, you will often see a key labeled .com when you are at a point in using a program where you are likely to enter a Web URL or an email address.

▶ **Offering external keyboards.** Unlike the iPhone, the iPad offers external keyboard support. Apple itself offers two keyboard options, and almost any Bluetooth keyboard works with iPad.

TIP: **External Keyboard Cursor Keys**
Since the iPad doesn't support a mouse, the cursor keys that you find on an external keyboard can be a very valuable feature of such a device.

In this lesson, I'll emphasize typing information using the onscreen keyboard. You will need to develop onscreen keyboarding skills to get the most out of your iPad. However, it's good to be aware of the extent to which this requirement is reduced by software, and avoidable by extra hardware, if you need it.

Using the Onscreen Keyboard

The onscreen keyboard comes up any time you need to enter text. It covers about half the screen in portrait mode, and about a third in landscape mode. In landscape mode, the onscreen keyboard is nearly as wide as a laptop's physical keyboard. However, the use of screen space by the onscreen keyboard (in either landscape or portrait mode) can interfere with your ability to see things onscreen that you need for text entry (such as when you're replying to an email).

Using the onscreen keyboard is a more interactive process than typing with a regular keyboard. The iPad is constantly watching what you're typing, correcting misspellings, offering predictive suggestions for you to choose from, and learning as you use it.

The following is a list of keys to successfully enter regular text, as shown in Figure 3.1—upper and lowercase letters, the comma, period, exclamation point, or question mark:

1. To bring up the onscreen keyboard, press in a text entry area.

2. Depending on the size of your fingers, the way you are supporting the iPad, and your need to see text or other content onscreen, you may prefer typing in landscape mode or portrait mode. Try both, and use the one that works best for you. The onscreen keyboard as it appears in landscape mode is shown in Figure 3.2.

3. To type lowercase text, a comma, or a period, press the appropriate keys on the onscreen keyboard to type. Note that, depending

FIGURE 3.1   The main onscreen keyboard, shown as it appears in portrait mode.

FIGURE 3.2   The main onscreen keyboard in landscape mode.

on the app, there may be a key with .com on it for entering URLs, or other special keys that fit the current app.

4. To type capital letters, the ! symbol, or the ? symbol, press Shift and then the letter. Or press Shift, hold, and then slide your finger to the letter; Shift is retained for that one letter.

5. Double-press the Shift key to turn it blue, meaning Caps Lock is on. Press the Shift key once to remove Caps Lock. (If Caps Lock doesn't work, or to turn it off if you don't like it, see the Settings, as described in Lesson 5, "Customizing General Settings for Your iPad.")

6. To type characters that aren't on the keyboard, such as accented vowels used in many non-English languages, rest your finger on the related letter or symbol. A floating menu of alternative versions or the character appears, as shown previously in Figure 3.1.

7. To delete the previously typed character, press the backspace key.

8. To end a sentence with a period, double-press the spacebar. The iPad automatically inserts a period and a space instead of two spaces.

For entering numbers and punctuation, or other special characters, do the following:

1. For numbers and some special characters (0-9 - / : ; ( ) $ & @ ' "), plus the four special characters found on all keyboards (. , ? !), press the 123 key, or number key (shown in Figure 3.3).

FIGURE 3.3   The Numbers keyboard in portrait mode.

2. For special characters ([ ] { } # % ^ * + = _ | ~ < > £), plus
quotes (' ") found on both special characters keyboards, plus the
four special characters found on all keyboards (. , ? !), press the
#+= key, or symbol key (shown in Figure 3.4). (Some characters
are mentioned here again because those characters are available
on multiple keyboards.)

FIGURE 3.4   The Symbols keyboard in portrait mode.

Getting to the number keys and symbol keys is a hassle, as is trying to
remember which special keys are on which keyboard. Practice will help,
and so will little workarounds, such as typing an ellipsis (...) instead of a
dash in notes to yourself, so you don't need to switch keyboards just for
one character.

There are some things you can do relating to text entry beyond the standard
keyboard, number keyboard and symbol keyboard, such as the following:

► **Use international keyboards.** Add access to international keyboards, as described in Lesson 5. Press and hold the Next
Keyboard key (which doesn't appear if there is only one main
keyboard set up).

► **Put the keyboard away.** Press the button in the lower right that
looks like a keyboard to put the keyboard away. Press in the text
entry area again to bring it back.

► **Lock the screen.** Having screen content shift orientations is con-
fusing, but having the keyboard keep changing orientations is

maddening. Use the Screen Lock switch, described in Lesson 1, "Introducing iPad," to prevent this.

▶ **Make a lap desk.** If you have the iPad case from Apple (see Lesson 1), you can fold it to create an angled support for the iPad that functions like a lap desk.

Using External Keyboards

The iPad has several options for using an external keyboard, as follows:

▶ Using the iPad Keyboard Dock from Apple (see Lesson 1)

▶ Using the Apple Wireless Keyboard from Apple (see Lesson 1)

▶ Using a wireless Bluetooth keyboard from another provider

TIP: **Get into Good Habits**

Try to develop a habitual way of entering text, using either portrait mode or landscape mode for most or all of your typing work. Good typing requires muscle memory, and the orientation of the screen has a big effect on where the keys are. So having a habitual setting improves your ability to type quickly without thinking.

TIP: **Making the Keyboard Go Away**

After you put the iPad in the iPad keyboard dock, or establish a Bluetooth connection with an external keyboard (see Lesson 4, "Getting Connected to Wi-Fi, 3G, and Bluetooth"), the onscreen keyboard disappears.

The external keyboard gives you several advantages, as follows:

▶ Rapid entry of text, digits, and symbols.

▶ Rapid movement of the insertion point or focus point for viewing and selection using cursor keys.

▶ Control of system functions, such as brightness, media playback, and sound volume, on the keyboards.

For keyboards not designed for use with the iPad, some of the keys may not be supported by the iPad.

CAUTION: **Getting the Keyboard Back**

If you use an external keyboard, the onscreen keyboard disappears. It may remain hidden even after you turn off the external keyboard or take it out of range. If this happens, turn off Bluetooth in the Settings app (see Lesson 4 for details).

External keyboards available at this writing don't provide mouse-type functionality nor help in making selections. Many onscreen functions therefore still require you to touch the screen directly.

Inserting Text Using the Interactive Dictionary

The iPad suggests corrections or completed versions of words you're typing. This function is called the Dictionary, but there are no definitions in this Dictionary. It's just to support fast and accurate text entry.

The Dictionary automatically replaces "bad" words with "good" alternatives that it suggests. (This is called Auto-Correction, and you can turn it off in the General area of the Settings, under Keyboard, if you want.) This is marvelous when it works, which for most people seems to be most of the time. It's a tremendous pain when it doesn't work, however, and replaces your carefully chosen rare or foreign word with an incorrect alternative. (For instance, if you're caring enough to want to send "besos" in an email note—"kisses" in Spanish—the Dictionary may replace it with "besis.")

The Dictionary also "learns." It gradually promotes suggestions that you use, and replaces suggestions you reject with the word you actually use.

I recommend that you use the Dictionary as follows:

▶ **Inspect the suggestion.** Type the first few characters of a longer word—I suggest typing three or four characters—then look at what suggestion the Dictionary has made. If it's not correct, add characters up to the end of the word, checking to see if the suggestion updates to the correct word.

▶ **Accept the suggestion.** If and when the suggestion is correct, accept the suggestion by pressing space, a punctuation mark, or the return character—just as if you had completed typing the word.

▶ **Reject the suggestion.** If you finish typing the entire word and the suggestion is incorrect, press the suggestion before pressing space, a punctuation mark, or the return character. Pressing the suggestion dismisses it. The Dictionary gradually learns to offer you the word you've typed when you start typing the same initial characters again.

To get the most out of Dictionary, I suggest that you develop an active strategy for using it. The goal is to type as little as possible, use the Dictionary as much as possible now, and train the Dictionary as much as possible for the future.

Editing with Cut, Copy, and Paste

One of the great challenges of touchscreens—indeed, a source of great inadequacy with all computers, until the mouse came along—has always been editing text. Editing requires fine control to specify the starting and stopping points for the selection, followed by quick access to options to choose the right one. Perfect for a mouse; difficult just about any other way.

The iPad has perhaps the best touchscreen version of cut, copy, and paste to date, but it still takes time and practice to use correctly. Here's how to do it:

1. Double-tap a word to select it.

The word appears with three controls: two selection markers called "grab bars," one at the beginning and one at the end, and a menu of options, as shown in Figure 3.5.

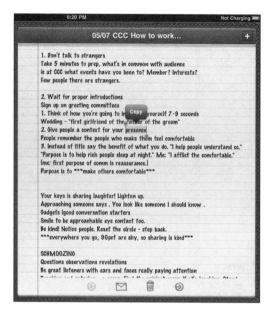

FIGURE 3.5 Mark the insertion starting and ending points.

The menu has different options depending on whether the text is editable or not. For editable text, such as in an email or Notes document that you're working on, it will include Cut, Copy, and Replace, plus Paste if there is an existing selection that you can paste in. (In this case, Replace refers to replacing a word with a similar word from the Dictionary. It does not mean "Replace with previously copied text"; Paste does that.)

2. To act on the selection, tap one of the options from the menu.

3. To change the selection, tap the blue button on the starting or ending grab bar.

   A magnifying glass appears, as shown in Figure 3.6.

4. While continuing to hold, drag your finger to move around the magnifying glass and, thereby, the grab bar. Release to set the new beginning or ending point of the selection.

5. To cancel the selection, press anywhere in the text.

   For editable text, a new insertion point appears where you tap.

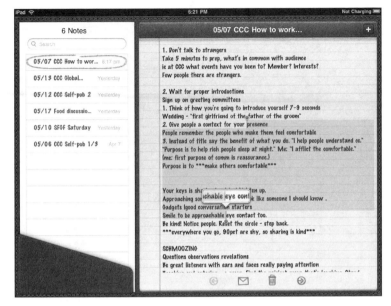

FIGURE 3.6   Use the magnifying glass to find your selection beginning or ending point.

Using Multi-Touch

The iPad screen supports the sophisticated use of a technology called multi-touch. Multi-touch includes direct manipulation of onscreen objects by touch, as well as various special commands, called gestures, also specified by touch.

Multi-touch enables you to use gestures on the screen's surface to indicate commands to the system software or an application. A multi-touch gesture is a specific way of touching the screen to get a specific result. For instance, moving your finger rapidly across the screen—"swiping—can move you to the next screen, showing an additional pane (on the Home screen) or the next album (in the iPod app). Putting two fingers onscreen and bringing them together (pinching) zooms in when using the Maps app; the opposite gesture zooms out.

The advantages of multi-touch include its speed, directness, and ease of use. Most multi-touch gestures seem obvious, and you may indeed find yourself using them without really thinking about it. However, it's worth taking the time to be aware of the controls available on the iPad, including multi-touch controls.

You should also be aware of differences in how multi-touch is implemented among apps. For instance, some apps that deal with multiple data items, such as Notes with its separate notes, don't allow swiping between them. (Swiping is defined later in this lesson.) Instead, you use arrow icons onscreen. You may have to experiment sometimes to find out which multi-touch gestures are supported by the app you're using.

Opening and Moving Among Applications

Applications on the iPad are commonly referred to as "apps," a name taken from the famous App Store that offers various Apple and third-party applications for the iPhone and iPad.

To open an app, start from the Home screen. Pressing the icon of the app you want opens the app.

To return to the Home screen, press the Home button, which will close the current app. However, some background services may continue. For instance, a song that you start in iPod can continue playing while you use another app.

Scrolling, Swiping, and Flicking

To move directly to the top of a list or a page, tap the status bar at the top of the screen. The options are scrolling, swiping, and flicking:

▶ *Scrolling*—moving up and down in a page or list by using a control called a "scroll bar"—is a commonly used function among computer applications. On the iPad, using multi-touch, you scroll by dragging your finger up and down on the screen. The iPad recognizes the gesture as distinct from selection, which is also done by touching the screen, but without the up-and-down, dragging motion.

▶ *Swiping* is an additional multi-touch function. Swiping is done by dragging the current screen left or right. The current screen content is replaced by the page or item that is "next to" the current one among the data items managed by the app.

The choice of what is "next to" the current item is determined by the application. For instance, in the Photos app, if you have a folder of photos open, you can view one, and then move to other photos in the folder by swiping. In Maps and Safari, you move among currently open maps or web pages, respectively, by swiping.

▶ *Flicking* is a quick, repeated scrolling or swiping gesture. Use flicking to move through a list or among items quickly.

▶ To select an item, press and hold it. This might cause a word to be selected, a song to play, or detailed information about an item (such as a contact) to appear.

After you select an item, a Back button (left-pointing curved arrow) may appear in the upper-left corner of the screen. Press the Back button to return to the list.

Zooming In and Out

Zooming in and out of various data items is done in two ways, as follows:

▶ **Pinching and spreading.** A pinching gesture zooms into an item, such as a map. To pinch, place two fingertips onscreen, some distance apart, and then bring them together. You will zoom into the item—a smaller area of the item will expand to fill the screen, enabling you to see greater detail.

▶ **Double-press and pressing with two fingers.** In many items, such as web pages, it can be useful to be able to quickly zoom in or out by a predetermined amount. In some apps, you can double-press (press twice quickly) onscreen to quickly zoom in by a predetermined amount. To zoom back out, you press once, with two fingers at the same time.

Summary

In this lesson, you learned how to enter text from the iPad screen using the onscreen keyboard, the Dictionary, and external keyboards. You also learned how to use multi-touch on the iPad screen. In the next lesson, you learn how to get and stay connected to the Internet and to external devices as much as possible, using Wi-Fi, 3G, and Bluetooth.

LESSON 4

Getting Connected to Wi-Fi, 3G, and Bluetooth

This lesson helps you learn how to get connected—and stay connected—to Wi-Fi hot spots; to 3G cellphone data coverage, if your iPad has 3G support; and to Bluetooth when (and only when) you need it.

Deciding How to Connect

Wi-Fi is the preferred way to connect your iPad to the Internet. It's also, usually, the only way for those of us who own an iPad Wi-Fi model rather than an iPad Wi-Fi+3G model.

Wi-Fi is another name for a wireless local area network, or WLAN. A WLAN works via "hot spots," the name for a wireless router that sends out and receives radio waves that are modulated to send and receive data to the Internet.

Wi-Fi hotspots are becoming nearly ubiquitous in some people's lives. There's a high likelihood that you have Wi-Fi access both at home and at work. You may also be able to get on Wi-Fi for free at friends' homes, on school campuses, in coffee shops, and even in meeting places. There's also paid Wi-Fi access in airports, additional cafes, and covering broad areas of cities. So, Wi-Fi access may be enough for you and your iPad.

When you're in hot spot range, Wi-Fi is fast and reliable—rock solid in comparison to 3G coverage. It also uses less power than 3G. Although you should use Wi-Fi as often as possible, having what's called 3G cellphone data coverage is also very valuable.

Exactly how valuable? Well, Apple charges $130 more, at this writing, for a 3G model than for an otherwise comparable Wi-Fi-only iPad. Plus, data coverage costs $15 a month for limited use (up to 250MB of data transferred) or $30 a month for unlimited use. You can cancel or restart the option at any point, but then, of course, you're not getting the use of the feature you paid extra to have available.

The two-year cost of the 3G option plus coverage, if you subscribe continuously, is $490 for limited use or $850 for unlimited use, roughly doubling the total cost of your iPad.

Bluetooth is very different from Wi-Fi, and it's normally used to connect to nearby devices, not to the Internet. Bluetooth is a very limited-range communications protocol that's used to link your iPad to devices such as keyboards and mice without the need for wires. However, you do need to turn off Bluetooth when you're not using it, both to save power and to close a potential open door for hackers who want your device's data and connections.

NOTE: **Getting 3G on a Wi-Fi iPad**

If you buy a Wi-Fi-only iPad, there's still a way to get online via 3G and other cellular network data services. A device called a MiFi receives a cellular network signal and uses it to create a portable hotspot. You can then connect up to five devices-iPads, laptops, and smartphones included-to the hotspot. Although the price is a bit more than the iPad 3G option, the MiFi is more flexible, and can help prevent you from experiencing "buyer's regret" for buying the Wi-Fi-only iPad instead of a 3G model. Some cell phones also have the capability to act as a hotspot of this type built-in. Check your current cellphone to see if it has this capability, and also look for it in the features list of any phone you're considering buying.

Connecting via Wi-Fi

Wi-Fi is the best way to connect to the Internet, as described at the beginning of this lesson. It can be a hassle to find and log into the nearest hotspot, but the following are a few reasons you should do so whenever possible, even if you have a 3G iPad, and a fast data connection seems to be available:

▶ **Speed.** The transfer speeds you experience via Wi-Fi vary, but are generally significantly faster than even the best and most reliable 3G connection.

▶ **Reliability.** 3G connections are unreliable in many areas, a situation that's only getting worse as devices like the iPad encourage increasing use of 3G data transfer. (See the 3G section later in the lesson.)

TIP: **Look for Wi-Fi Access**

Take the time to find out where Wi-Fi is available as you move about with your iPad, to get Wi-Fi passwords where needed, and to find out about free and paid Wi-Fi services that may be a good lifeline if you need an Internet connection (even if you have 3G capability, for the reasons stated previously). Wi-Fi access helps you get the most out of your iPad.

▶ **Power use.** Wi-Fi uses less power than 3G, and being connected to Wi-Fi enables you to turn off cellphone data network access, saving more power. Using a bit less electricity is good for the environment, even when you're not worried about running out of battery power.

Follow these steps to join a nearby Wi-Fi network from your iPad:

1. Choose Settings->Wi-Fi. Use the slider to turn on Wi-Fi.

A list of available networks appears, as shown in Figure 4.1. A lock icon appears for networks that require a password. Some networks require you to pay for access.

A symbol with one to three arcs filled in indicates the signal strength for each network. (You'll notice that the lowest-strength networks tend to appear and disappear from the list as the level

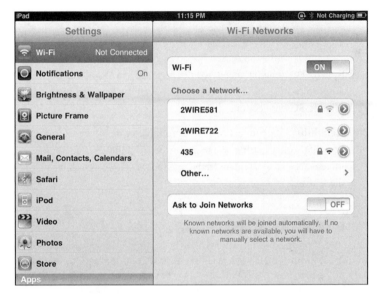

FIGURE 4.1   Log into the best available network.

of local interference changes and makes them just reachable, or just out of reach.)

2. Wait a moment to allow available networks to appear, and then press to select a network. If no password is required, you'll join the network immediately.

   If a password is required to join the network, a request for the password appears, as shown in Figure 4.2. Passwords are sometimes available on the wireless router itself or from a system administrator or customer service person nearby.

3. Enter the password, if required. You'll join the network. Also, your iPad will remember the password, and you'll join the network immediately whenever you're in range.

4. To view technical details of the network, press the blue arrow next to the network.

FIGURE 4.2   Enter the password for secured networks.

Technical details of the network appear, as shown in Figure 4.3. For systems that you've previously logged into, an option to forget the network also appears.

5. To forget a network—that is, to have your iPad erase the stored password for it—press the Forget This Network button. The iPad erases the stored password for this network. This prevents your iPad from automatically joining this network when you are in range, allowing you to give preference to another nearby network simply by visiting it (and not forgetting it afterward). In the future, your iPad automatically joins the most recently used network out of those in range that it has previously joined.

FIGURE 4.3   Ignore the technical details in most cases and just forget this network, or don't.

The specific instructions for managing individual wireless networks can be summed up differently as a procedure for automatically connecting to the best available hotspot, as follows:

▶ Inspect the available networks.

▶ Decide which one you want to prefer.

▶ Join it. Your iPad will then automatically keep connecting to this network first whenever the network is in range.

▶ To avoid automatically joining a network, forget it, as described in the preceding steps.

TIP: **The Status Bar Shows Your Connection**

The connection strength for the currently connected Wi-Fi network is shown in the status bar. See the Using the Onscreen Keyboard section of Lesson 3, "Editing Text and Using Multi-Touch," for more information about status bar icons.

Connecting via 3G

The name 3G for some iPad models is a bit of a misnomer. It really means that your iPad can connect to the Internet using cellular data networks at speeds up to 3G. The other connection options are GPRS (2G) and, in some countries, EDGE (2.5G). So, 3G really means "cellular data networks at the fastest available speed, up to 3G."

CAUTION: **Look Out for Some Free Networks**

Some networks have no access restrictions due to being deliberately made freely available, or accidentally being left freely available, or being set up and run for malicious purposes such as data stealing. It's illegal to knowingly tap into a free network that doesn't expressly permit public access, and dangerous to the security of your data and iPad software to risk tapping into a malicious one. So, don't join a free network unless and until you know who's offering it and that they're trustworthy.

This is great as of the iPad's introduction in the spring of 2010, but 4G networks were already beginning to be discussed at that time. Soon the coming thing will be 4G, which is faster and has higher capacity. So, 3G means "the best" at this writing, but it will mean something less in the near future.

Any of the types of data network connection is adequate for background tasks like downloading email or broadcasting your location to social networking sites that use it for various purposes. However, interactive tasks like web surfing and getting directions benefit greatly from the higher speed and responsiveness of EDGE or, particularly, 3G—when it works reliably.

You can expect to get a GPRS data connection just about anywhere you can get a wireless signal adequate for a phone call. EDGE and 3G connections are progressively more limited in coverage area, and are therefore unavailable in some areas.

Unfortunately for all concerned, the very usefulness and popularity of 3G means that, where there is coverage, the network is often overcrowded in certain areas. Poor implementation of all the networks means that service doesn't gracefully degrade from one level of service to the next among cellphone voice service and the data network connections—3G, EDGE, and GPRS.

Instead, every device fights for 3G bandwidth for every application, truly high-priority or not. When the 3G service gets overcrowded, cellphone calls can't be made or get dropped, web page downloads freeze, and more. Unfortunately, you can't make your 3G iPad use a lesser protocol if you're having problems.

TIP: **Use Wi-Fi When You Can**

In some areas, 3G connections are unavailable, or slow and unreliable, and 3G uses additional battery power. Get in the habit of using Wi-Fi whenever possible, and only use 3G when you have to.

There are two requirements for 3G service on your iPad, as follows:

▶ A built-in 3G radio receiver, which is built into iPad Wi-Fi+3G models—and unavailable on iPad Wi-Fi-only models.

▶ 3G data service, available on a month-by-month basis, as described at the beginning of this lesson. In the U.S., at this writing, 3G data service is only available from AT&T, the cellular phone and data service provider for the iPhone—and famous for its spotty 3G performance in major urban areas.

You may want to check 3G coverage in the areas where you live, work, and frequently visit to find out what the promised level of 3G coverage is—and then talk to people in the affected areas to learn about the level of support you can actually expect.

When traveling outside of your provider's service area, you may be able to get data roaming support—but if you just log on and start using it on arrival, it's likely to be very, very expensive. Check with your home provider before travelling and see if you can get a reasonably-priced roaming plan before you leave your usual service area.

CAUTION: **Turn Off Data Roaming**

To avoid data roaming charges, make sure the Data Roaming setting is turned off, as described here. If you do turn on the Data Roaming setting so as to use roaming services for some period of time, be sure to turn it back off afterward.

Follow these steps to manage the use of cellular data networking service on your iPad Wi-Fi+3G:

1. To set up or stop a cellular data plan, tap the Settings icon, and choose Cellular Data and then Cellular Data Plan. Follow the onscreen instructions. (You will need to obtain a micro-SIM card before using cellular data.) Visit the same Settings area if and when you want to stop your plan.

2. To turn off data roaming, tap the Settings icon and choose Cellular Data. If data roaming is On, turn the slider to Off.

3. Turn off all iPad radio transmitters—Wi-Fi, cellular data, and GPS—by tapping Airplane Mode in Settings (this is only available on iPad Wi-Fi+3G). On some airplanes, you may then be allowed to turn on Wi-Fi, not 3G, in order to use onboard Wi-Fi services, possibly at an extra charge.

Using Bluetooth

Bluetooth—described at the beginning of this lesson—is used for peripheral devices, such as a wireless keyboard or wireless headphones, at distances of up to a few feet.

In order to use your iPad's Bluetooth connection with a specific device, you have to pair them.

Follow these steps to pair a Bluetooth device with the iPad:

1. Look at the instructions for the device in question and take the steps needed to make it discoverable.

These steps are usually fairly simple. On the Apple Bluetooth keyboard, for instance, you simply turn on the keyboard. Other devices may require some combination of button presses. Check the printed or online documentation for the device.

2. In the Settings application, tap General, and then Bluetooth, and slide the Bluetooth option to On.

The iPad will display a list of devices it has successfully paired with and start searching for new, discoverable Bluetooth devices.

3. The iPad will discover the nearby device and ask you to confirm that it is the appropriate one by entering some kind of code.

For instance, for the Apple Bluetooth keyboard, the iPad will ask you to enter a PIN by typing on the numeric keys of the device, as shown in Figure 4.4.

4. Quickly complete the requested step.

If you don't complete the step in time, the process will time out, and you'll have to restart.

FIGURE 4.4   The iPad asks for help in pairing.

5. If you complete the step requested on time, the device will pair with the iPad. If you fail to complete the step requested on time, turn off Bluetooth and then start over.

Once successful, you will not have to complete the pairing process again in normal use, although the device may "forget" that it is paired if it loses power. In this case, repeat the pairing process.

6. Once you have paired a device, if you stop using it, you should clear it from the iPad's memory. To do this, choose the device from the list on the Bluetooth screen. On the screen that appears, choose Forget this Device.

The device will be unpaired. If you want to re-pair it, you may need to remove the power connection and/or batteries from the device so that it forgets it was previously paired and gives you the opportunity to re-pair it.

CAUTION: **Keep Bluetooth Off**

Bluetooth connections are a potential target of hackers who can move through public places, looking for data they can steal over Bluetooth. Bluetooth also uses additional battery power. Be sure to turn off Bluetooth whenever you're not using it.

Summary

In this lesson, you learned how to connect to the Internet using Wi-Fi and, if available on your iPad model, 3G. You also learned how to pair Bluetooth devices to your iPad. In the next lesson, you will learn how to customize settings for your iPad.

LESSON 5

Customizing General Settings for Your iPad

This lesson explains how to use the iPad's General Settings to manage the overall system, including storage, international and language settings, restrictions, additional keyboards, and more.

Managing iPad Settings

Settings often hold many secrets to getting a device to work well and to fit the way you use it. The iPad's settings, however, are somewhat different than the settings on other computing devices, with much less under the control of the user than on other systems. With the iPad, you are unable to set the system font or the size of displayed characters. (Though you can, in some cases, zoom.) Neither data files nor program files are directly accessible. In this sense, the iPad is much less a toy—something you play with for its own sake—than a tool, though a multi-talented one.

The iPad does have some helpful features among its settings, though. These include very flexible use of onscreen and external keyboards for a variety of languages and character sets, as well as strong accessibility options.

It's still valuable to review the available settings on the iPad to see what you can do, but equally, to see what you can't do. Table 5.1 summarizes the available options. So, learn what is available, and then enjoy getting the most out of your iPad as you use it.

TABLE 5.1   General Settings Described in This Lesson

Category	Functionality
About	Lists the number of items from different media types on your iPad, and shows available capacity and technical details.
Sounds	Turns sound on and off for mail received and sent, calendar, lock, and keyboard.
Auto-Lock	Option to turn on the screen saver and require a button slide to allow access after a delay that you specify.
Passcode Lock	Option to lock iPad and require a four-digit code to allow access after a delay that you specify.
Restrictions	Option to restrict access to many built-in iPad apps and to mature content for music, movies, TV shows, and apps.
Home	Specifies what a double-click on the Home button does, whether iPod controls appear onscreen, and what gets searched by Searchlight.
Date & Time	Sets time format, time zone, and system date and time.
Keyboard	Sets keyboard interactivity options; add onscreen and external keyboards in various formats.
International	Sets language; set region format for system display of dates, times, and phone numbers.
Battery %	Option to display specific percentage of battery life remaining or not.
Reset	Option to reset all settings; to erase all settings; or to reset settings specifically for networking, the keyboard dictionary, the Home screen layout, or location warnings.

NOTE: **Spend Time with Settings**

This lesson only summarizes some of the settings and their effects. Take the time to look through and experiment with settings to understand them and their effects in more detail.

About

The About area (see Figure 5.1) contains details that help you manage storage on your device, along with some other not-so-important details.

FIGURE 5.1   The iPad offers you a storage overview and system specifics.

The important areas for managing storage are as follows:

- ▶ **Songs.** Songs in MP3 format take up about 1MB per minute of time in the song. So, a 30-minute symphony would take up more storage than a 3-minute pop song.

- ▶ **Videos.** Videos can be short clips or long movies, highly compressed or HD-quality. Higher-quality videos take up about 10MB per 1 minute of time in the video. (That means a 100-minute, high-quality movie takes up about 1GB.)

- ▶ **Photos.** Photos can be high-resolution monsters of 5MB or even unprocessed image files that take up 15MB each. They can also be small, compressed versions that just take up 100KB or so.

- ▶ **Applications.** Apps vary widely (and wildly). An app can be almost unnoticeably small, or 100MB in size, or even larger, especially if it incorporates a lot of video. Additionally, an app size increases as you add to the data managed by the app—for instance, when you create notes in the Notes app.

▶ **Capacity.** This is the "budget" on your iPad for data—songs, videos, photos, apps, and their data. The system software and data takes up approximately 2GB, so you are left with almost the full use of your 16GB, 32GB, or 64GB iPad.

▶ **Available.** The amount of storage capacity remaining.

Unfortunately, the iPad doesn't offer a summary of your storage use. You can only estimate from this screen.

In addition to the storage-related information, the About area has some potentially important information that you're less likely to need directly, as follows:

▶ **Version; Model; Serial Number; Wi-Fi Address; Bluetooth.** Specific technical information that you may need to look up for technical support or other purposes.

▶ **Legal; Regulatory.** Apple is required to make certain information available on the machine. This is where you'll find it.

Sounds

Sounds enables you to set an overall range for system-level sounds—from completely muted to full volume—and to set which system events trigger sounds. The choices are as follows:

▶ **New Mail and Sent Mail.** Get alerted as emails come in and go out.

▶ **Calendar Alerts.** Help calendar items get your attention.

▶ **Lock Sounds.** When you lock the screen orientation on your iPad, for instance, you can hear a satisfying click.

▶ **Keyboard Clicks.** This gives you audio feedback as to whether you touched no keys, one, or more than one.

Each option has its own set sounds. To hear the different sounds, use the slider to turn an option off, then on. As you turn on the option, you'll hear its assigned sound. Then you are able to choose which setting you prefer.

Network

Network has two sets of settings: VPN, or a Virtual Private Network, and Wi-Fi.

A Virtual Private Network gives users the feeling of being directly connected to a company or other organization's network while using the publicly available Internet as "plumbing" for carrying data and control information. This requires a lot of technical settings that you won't normally need to be concerned with.

The organization that supplies your VPN should also supply setup information. Or, your organization may physically take your iPad from you, set it up on your VPN, test that everything works, and return it to you, along with instructions on how to use it effectively and securely.

The second set of settings is for Wi-Fi. Wi-Fi settings are more commonly accessed through the Wi-Fi Settings option at the top of the Settings list, which presents exactly the same screens and options as if you come into the Wi-Fi settings via the Network option. Wi-Fi settings are discussed in the previous lesson.

Bluetooth

Bluetooth settings help you attach, or "pair," Bluetooth devices to your iPad, and manage security and power usage by turning off Bluetooth when not in active use. Bluetooth settings are described in the previous lesson under the heading, "Using Bluetooth."

Location Services

Location Services includes the GPS radio in your iPad and the software that supports it. See Lesson 10, "Working with Maps," for more on GPS and how it works in conjunction with Wi-Fi and, if available, 3G on your iPad.

> CAUTION: **Turn Off GPS When You Can**
> The GPS radio in the iPad 3G uses a considerable amount of power, so turn it off when possible. You'll want to have it on,

> though, when using the Maps app or geo-aware apps and web sites.

An app or web site will not necessarily tell you to turn on your system's GPS radio to provide information—it will simply provide geo-aware services if information location is available, and not provide them (or not provide them as well) if it isn't. Therefore, it's up to you to figure out when you need Location Services turned on (for more functionality) or off (to save power).

Auto-Lock

Auto-Lock is the function that controls the frequency of the unlocking operation you go through when you use your iPad. There isn't a security aspect to this; it just turns off the screen, saving power and providing privacy for you with regard to the screen's contents. Auto-Lock also prevents you from accidentally entering commands or characters into the iPad when you're not intending to use it. (For instance, if it gets jostled in your bag when you're carrying it.)

> CAUTION: **Save Your Screen!**
>
> If you allow the same image to remain on your iPad screen repeatedly, a "ghost" of it might become permanently etched into your screen's phosphors, interfering with your use and enjoyment of your iPad. Use Auto-Lock to turn off the screen after a few minutes of non-use.

The Auto-Lock option has several possible settings: 2 minutes, 5 minutes, 10 minutes, 15 minutes, and Never. Choose the one that makes the most sense for you. In most cases, you should avoid the Never option, as it can too easily lead to wasting power and to screen burn-in.

Passcode Lock

The iPad Passcode Lock setting is similar to a feature found on personal computers, and also on some mobile phones. After a period of non-use, the system becomes blocked, and a password is required to re-access it.

Passcodes make a great deal of sense for personal computers, which are likely to contain financial and other highly confidential information for yourself and/or your company. An iPad, however, can be used in different ways.

Your iPad may have just as much confidential information, access to your email, and so on as a personal computer. However, if your only intent is to load your iPad with things like television episodes or music, the security implications of someone accessing it may not be truly dire.

In addition, many people find passcodes (and even Auto-Lock, described in the previous section) a tremendous hassle and annoyance; others find it normal and reassuring. Consider your own security needs and comfort level before deciding whether and how to use Passcode Lock.

The Passcode Lock setting has several options, as follows:

▶ **Turn Passcode On/Off.** This option turns the entire Passcode feature off or on. See Figure 5.2 for the entry box iPad uses to enable you to enter a passcode.

FIGURE 5.2   You can use passcodes for your system and for app restrictions.

▶ **Change Passcode.** Use this option to change the actual passcode you enter. Be very careful not to create a passcode you then forget, as you will have a great deal of trouble getting access to your iPad if it's locked and you don't have the passcode.

▶ **Require Passcode.** With this option, you have the ability to specify the amount of time that your system is unused before passcode protection goes into effect. The available options are: Immediately; After 1 minute, 5 minutes, or 15 minutes; and After 1 hour or 4 hours.

CAUTION: **Use a Memorable Passcode**

Be sure you can remember your passcode after you set it up, or change it.

▶ **Picture Frame.** This feature enables you to view stored photos on your machine while it's locked. It can be turned on or off.

▶ **Erase Data.** Choosing this option specifies that all data on your iPad will be erased after 10 failed passcode attempts. Use caution before choosing this option, as the results are permanent.

CAUTION: **Look Out for Dodgy Photos**

Think twice about all the photos stored on your machine before turning on Picture Frame. Some photos may become inappropriate if displayed in a business environment, and can even be grounds for disciplinary action or termination, so use discretion.

Restrictions

Restrictions settings enable you to control purchasing ability for apps and web sites, as well as content restrictions for media, including music, movies, TV shows, and even apps.

To enable Restrictions, press the Enable Restrictions button; the screen will then display possible restrictions, as shown in Figure 5.3. You'll be asked to enter a four-digit passcode for restrictions. As with Passcode Lock, be very careful not to set a passcode you might forget; it could cause you significant expense and hassle to override it.

FIGURE 5.3 You can enter a range of restrictions for your iPad.

Some of the built-in apps are potentially troublesome because they can be used to access content not suitable for children. You can turn off several potentially troublesome apps entirely: Safari, YouTube, iTunes, the App Store (and the ability to install apps), and Location services. Once the app is disabled, its icon is removed from the Home screen.

You also have the ability to specify what content you would like to allow. The following is a list of settings relating to content that you can change:

▶ **In-App Purchases.** A growing number of apps enable you to purchase upgraded functionality, additional episodes, and even additional items or character abilities in a game, all from within the app.

▶ **Ratings For.** This setting enables you to specify the country whose TV and movie ratings you want to use—Australia, Canada, France, Germany, Ireland, Japan, New Zealand, United Kingdom, or United States. Not all content will be rated in all jurisdictions.

▶ **Music & Podcasts.** You have the ability to allow or disallow content labeled Explicit.

▶ **Movies.** You may specify which level of movies to allow. For U.S. ratings, the levels are: Don't Allow Movies, G, PG, PG-13, R, NC-17, or Allow All Movies.

▶ **TV Shows.** With this Restriction setting, you can specify which level of TV shows to allow. For U.S. ratings, the levels are: Don't Allow TV Show, TV-Y, TV-Y7, TV-G, TV-PG, TV-14, TV-MA, or Allow All TV Shows.

▶ **Apps.** Adjusting this setting enables you to specify which level of apps to allow. The levels are: Don't Allow Apps, 4+, 9+, 12+, 17+, or Allow All Apps.

NOTE: **Watch Out for Racy Web Sites**

At this writing, apps are tightly restricted by Apple, so very little that might be considered obscene or offensive is allowed in apps. At the same time, a site such as Safari, being an unrestricted web browser, can allow you access to content that's obscene or offensive by almost anyone's definition. Web sites are also poorly labeled and regulated. Unfortunately, selective restricting within the sites you visit is not an available option.

Home

The Home settings area is an option in the General area of Settings, as shown in Figure 5.4. It enables you to specify what app shows up when you double-press the Home control and to manage specific settings for iPod controls and search results, as follows:

▶ **Home Button.** By double-clicking the Home button, you will be directed to the Home screen; to search for your iPad; or to the iPod app.

▶ **iPod Controls.** Specify whether to show iPod controls when playing music.

FIGURE 5.4   Home settings let you update a few different controls.

▶ **Search Results.** Specify which apps are included in searches of your iPad from the Spotlight page—Contacts, Applications, Music, Podcasts, Video, Audiobooks, Notes, Mail, and Calendar. Press and drag the list icon next to each app name to move that app up or down in the search results list.

Date & Time

With this function, you can turn on 24-hour (military) time, so your time appears as 2311 instead of 11:11pm. You also have the ability to set the time zone to your home city, which you may want to change when you are traveling outside of your usual time zone. If desired, you can also set the date and time directly.

Keyboard

The goal of the iPad's typing system is to enable you to type quickly, and even a bit carelessly, and still get good results. However, the adjustments that the iPad makes for you can be a bit annoying sometimes—and, if you like to take full control of getting the details right, even downright frustrating.

If you frequently use an external keyboard, and find that you're more accurate with it than with the onscreen keyboard, you may additionally want what you type to not be changed for you by the system software. That's because you're making fewer errors, so the adjustments the iPad makes are that much more likely to be causing, rather than fixing, errors.

Keyboard settings enable you to take back as much or as little control as you want to, as follows:

▶ **Auto-Correction.** This option controls whether entries are auto-corrected using the Dictionary. The Dictionary can be quite useful, but if you use a lot of unusual or specialist terms, or even custom abbreviations that tend to get auto-corrected into unintelligibility, you may want to turn off Auto-Correction.

▶ **Auto-Capitalization.** Use this option to control whether the first letter after a full stop is automatically capitalized.

▶ **Enable Caps Lock.** As on a physical keyboard, it's easy to accidentally enable Caps Lock on the iPad's onscreen keyboard. To avoid this problem, the default setting for Caps Lock is Off.

▶ **"." Shortcut.** This shortcut automatically converts a double-space (pressing the spacebar twice) to a period followed by a space. In combination with auto-capitalization, this creates a very easy way to end one sentence and start another, since the period at the end of one sentence, and the capital letter at the beginning of another, are automatically created simply by double-spacing.

You can also specify many different options for the onscreen keyboard and any external keyboard you want to use, as follows:

▶ **English keyboard.** Specify whether the default, English-language onscreen keyboard uses a classic QWERTY layout or a modified

AZERTY or QWERTZ layout. (You might give these a try if you're not familiar with them to see if they would work better for you.)

▶ **Hardware keyboard layout.** You can use many different kinds of external keyboards via Bluetooth. The layouts supported are U.S., Dvorak, U.S. International—PC, U.S. Extended, British, French, German, Spanish—ISO, Italian, Dutch, and Belgian.

You can also add additional onscreen keyboards to your iPad, as follows:

▶ **Add New Keyboard.** This button offers choices of Chinese (Simplified) Handwriting, Chinese (Simplified) Pinyin, Dutch, English (UK), Flemish, French, French (Canada), German, Italian, Japanese, Russian, and Spanish. You can add as many keyboards as you like.

▶ **Removing an onscreen keyboard.** Bring the list of keyboards onscreen in the Keyboard Settings area; then press Edit. A red Delete button will appear next to each keyboard. Press the Delete button for the keyboard you want to delete. If you chose to delete the English keyboard, the first keyboard listed will then become your default keyboard.

To access the additional onscreen keyboard(s) you have added, press the World key (globe icon) on your default keyboard. You can then switch between keyboards as needed.

TIP: **iPad Keyboards Are Easy**

Adding and using additional keyboards on iPad is easy. If you need to use ideographic characters, as with Chinese or Japanese, or to flexibly mix languages, it may be as easy as, or easier than, any other input method for which you could find the most simplistic option.

International

Choose the appropriate internationally compliant settings for your iPad, as follows:

▶ **Language.** Choose among Chinese, Dutch, English, French, German, Italian, Japanese, Russian, and Spanish.

▶ **Keyboards.** Choose keyboards and add external and onscreen keyboards, as described in the previous section.

▶ **Region format.** Set the region format for date, time, and phone number layout. For instance, for the UK, the formats for date, time, and phone number would appear as follows: Tuesday, 5 January 2010; 00:34; 07700 900202.

NOTE: **Use County-specific Formats**

The iPad supports dozens of region formats for dates, times, and phone numbers, including country-specific formats for Spanish-speaking and German-speaking countries, among others.

Accessibility

The iPad has a very strong set of accessibility options, and may be among the best options out there for addressing your needs for input and computing flexibility.

Battery Percentage

You have the option to display or to hide the battery percentage in the Status bar. Move the slider to see the effect: You are only hiding or displaying the numeric display, such as: 98%. The icon, which displays the approximate battery charge status and whether the device is plugged in, will remain.

Reset and Profile

You can reset several different groups of settings on your iPad to what they were when you first purchased your iPad, as follows:

▶ **Reset All Settings.** Choose this option to clear all preferences and settings you have entered. Unlike the next option, the Reset All Settings option does not erase app data such as Contacts and Calendar entries. Media, such as videos and songs, is also left intact.

▶ **Erase All Content and Settings.** Choose this option to clear all preferences and settings you have entered. Unlike the previous option, this option erases app data such as Contacts and Calendar entries, and media such as videos and songs. (Some of this information may be recovered if and when you synch with an external source for app data, or with iTunes, for media.)

▶ **Reset Network Settings.** Choose this option to make iPad "forget" any previously used network and VPN settings, except those installed by a configuration profile. Wi-Fi is turned off and then back on to disconnect you from any currently connected Wi-Fi network. Wi-Fi is left on, and the "Ask to Join Networks" setting is left on.

▶ **Reset Keyboard Dictionary.** As you use your iPad, the Dictionary adds a word whenever you reject a Dictionary suggestion and use another word instead. It then stops making the suggestion it had made before. Choose this option to reset the Dictionary, erasing all previously added words.

▶ **Reset Home Screen Layout.** Choose this option to return the Home screen layout to its original settings.

▶ **Reset Location Warnings.** Choose this option to erase any record of previously accepting requests for an app, such as Maps, to use the iPad's Location Services, as shown in Figure 5.5.

The Profiles list includes configuration profiles for VPN settings. To delete a profile, select it from the list under Profiles; then press Remove.

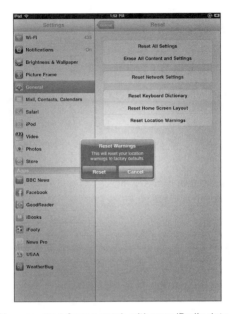

FIGURE 5.5   You can start from scratch with your iPad's data.

Summary

In this lesson, you learned how to use the iPad's General Settings to manage settings relating to the overall system, such as storage, international and language settings, content restrictions, and additional keyboards. In the next lesson I'll describe using the Web on your iPad.

LESSON 6

Using the Web on Safari

This lesson shows you how to surf the Web from the iPad using Apple's Safari browser, including viewing web pages, searching the Web, using bookmarks and web clips, and working around possible concerns with screen size and lack of Adobe Flash support. Surfing the Web requires an Internet connection; for information on getting connected, see Lesson 4, "Getting Connected to Wi-Fi, 3G, and Bluetooth."

> NOTE: **Fitting Sites on the iPad Screen**
> The iPad screen is slightly smaller than most screens in use today; its resolution is 1024 x 768 pixels, whereas most laptop screens today are 1280 x 800. Therefore, some web sites that are designed to take advantage of big screens will not quite fit onscreen on the iPad. Also, the iPad does not support Flash, a popular format for multimedia. So some Web multimedia won't work on your iPad.

Introducing Safari on iPad

Surfing the Web from the iPad using Apple's Safari browser is a highlight of using the device. For some people, it's *the* highlight. Because you hold the iPad in your hands and touch the screen directly, you interact with the Web differently than on a personal computer. And, because the iPad's screen is so large compared to the screen on a cellphone, the iPad experience is much better than that as well. Web surfing on the iPad is particularly (and impressively) flexible if you have an iPad Wi-Fi+3G model, rather than an iPad Wi-Fi only model. (See Lesson 4 for details.)

The iPad's 1024 x 768 screen resolution is generous compared to smart-phone screen sizes, including the iPhone's 480 x 320, but still a bit small for some web page layouts. Also, the iPad does not support Adobe Flash, which means that many cool multimedia features—and even the core func-tionality of some entire web sites—don't work at all on iPad. Despite these hassles, though, the iPad is a great web surfing machine.

Using Portrait and Landscape Modes

A preferred way to surf the Web with the iPad is to use it in portrait mode (like the way you would usually write on a letter-size or legal-size tablet of paper). Since web pages are most often designed and used in this kind of orientation, they look great rendered that way in a device you can easily hold in your hands. Many pages work well this way too.

One of the greatest things about using the iPad, though, is its "always upright" functionality—the page continuously rotates to follow the way that you're holding the device. There's no "wrong" way to hold an iPad, though. As with web pages, some content works better one way or the other.

This "always upright" functionality goes from being optional to becoming a necessity when using Safari and viewing web pages. The reason is sim-ple: Many web sites today are designed for widescreens, for instance, to fill, or almost fill, the 1280 x 800 resolution common on laptops. When you visit a widescreen-oriented web site with the iPad in portrait mode, the horizontal resolution is only 768 pixels, instead of, perhaps, 1280 pixels—a reduction of nearly half. Because of this, the page may not render very well at all. It may reflow into the much narrower space in a clumsy way, or you may need to zoom out to get a better view of the page.

At this writing, the InformIT site that publicizes Sams titles like the one you hold in your hand is one of these widescreen-oriented sites when viewed on a personal computer monitor. The site has a wide left-hand column that would, by itself, come close to filling the width of an old-fashioned 800 x 600-resolution personal computer monitor. It has an addi-tional column about half as large. If you narrow the window on a personal computer to about 800 pixels, not much changes—you just lose the right-hand column until you scroll sideways.

When viewed on the iPad in portrait mode, though, the site fits right in, as shown in Figure 6.1. It does this, though, by shrinking the text—perhaps to a level that's unreadable, or at least that isn't much fun to read.

FIGURE 6.1   Some screens shrink in the iPad's portrait mode.

Turn the iPad on its side, and suddenly, the text gets bigger, as shown in Figure 6.2. You don't get much depth, but what you do see is quite read-able. You might even find yourself using portrait mode to navigate around the site, and landscape mode for the parts you really want to read.

TIP: **Consider Using the Same Browser**

Consider using the same browser on your personal computer (or, if you have more than one, on all your personal computers) as well as on iPad, so you have a consistent experience on different sys-tems. The native iPad browser, Safari, is also the native browser on the Macintosh and the iPhone, and is available as a free download for Windows machines. An alternative, Opera, is available for multiple computer platforms and in an iPhone version that also runs on the iPad, albeit in an ugly, pixel-doubled mode.

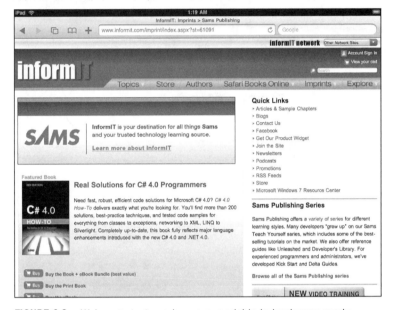

FIGURE 6.2   Web page text can be more readable in landscape mode.

Opening Web Pages

Opening a web page can be more difficult on an iPad than on a personal computer because web URLs are a mix of letters and special characters. Thus, entering them on your iPad can take longer than it would on a personal computer.

Here are a few pointers for entering a web address that can help speed up the process:

▶ **Finding the URL field.** Many web sites cause the URL field to be hidden. Scroll up or simply tap the status bar to bring the URL field onscreen even quicker.

▶ **Deleting the existing URL.** To get rid of a URL that's already in the address bar, tap the address field and then tap the X that appears. Get in the habit of doing this before you begin entering text, as it's annoying to struggle to enter a URL via text entry, only to find there's a jumbled mess in the URL field.

▶ **Using shortcuts.** When you begin entering a part of the URL you want, matching web addresses that you entered in the past will appear beneath the URL you're entering. Watch the list and pick out an appropriate one as soon as it appears.

▶ **Reducing text entry.** Consider going to any shortcut that matches the site you want—even if it's not the exact URL—and then navigating within the site to reach your desired web page, instead of typing the full URL.

TIP: **How Not to Open a New Page**

Some web links, such as search results, automatically open in a new page, closing the search results page. To override this behavior, press and hold on the link, and choose Open instead of Open in New Page.

▶ **Storing web pages.** You can open multiple pages by pressing the multi-page button. A list of currently open web pages appears (up to nine can be open at once), as shown in Figure 6.3. Tap New Page to save the previous web page for later re-use.

▶ **Searching the Web.** Press in the search area in the upper-right corner, enter the word or phrase you want, and then tap Search. When the search results appear, press on the area to open the result in a new window, or press and hold to get the option to open the result in the same window, replacing the search results.

▶ **Re-visiting web pages.** Press the multi-page button; then choose the previously visited web page you want from among the stored web pages. The effect of this is a lot like having nine web browser windows open at once.

FIGURE 6.3   Manage stored web pages for flexibility.

TIP: **Use History to Return to a Page**

You can use History, described later in the lesson, to quickly re-visit recently opened web pages. Use the multi-page function more strategically to hold sites that you may want to revisit multi-ple times over a longer session of using the iPad.

▶ **Closing unneeded web pages.** Treat the multi-page function as nine "slots" that you keep filled with web pages you want to revisit. To get rid of a stored web page, open up a slot and then press the X on the upper-left corner of the icon representing the page.

Zooming and Scrolling

The iPad screen is much larger than a smartphone screen. For instance, the iPad screen is about five times the size, in pixels, of an iPhone screen. It's about three-fourths the size of a typical wide-screen laptop, though, so you'll have to zoom and scroll sometimes to access content and to read text clearly.

To zoom and scroll in Safari, use the following gestures:

> ► **Zoom in or out by pinching.** Pinch or spread your fingers to move in and out of a web page.

> ► **Zoom in or out by pressing.** Double-press within a column on a web page to expand it (zoom in). Double-press again on an expanded column to compress it (zoom out).

> ► **Scroll a web page.** Press and drag up and down or sideways. The iPad detects that you're scrolling and doesn't follow any links that may be under your finger.

> ► **Scroll within a frame.** Press and drag with two fingers, not just one, up and down or sideways.

> ► **Go to the top.** Press the Status bar.

Navigating Web Pages

Careful navigating among web pages is particularly important on the iPad because the screen space and multitasking capability are both limited.

The following tips for navigating web pages thoroughly help you get the most out of the iPad and Safari:

> ► **Options for opening links.** You can see linking options by pressing and holding the link, as shown in Figure 6.4. A box with the destination URL (in very small type) and options will appear. Options may include Open, Open in New Page, Save Image (saves an image in the Photo Library), and Copy.

> ► **Stop loading the web page.** Press X in the address field.

> ► **Reload the page.** Press the reload arrow in the address field.

> ► **Move to the next or previous web page.** Press the left or right arrow in the address bar, if available.

FIGURE 6.4   Open up your options by pressing and holding a link.

▶ **Access current URL options.** Press + in the address field, causing options to appear, as shown in Figure 6.5. From among the
  options that appear, choose Add Bookmark, Add to Home Screen
  to save a "live" icon called a web clip to the Home screen, or
  Mail Link to this Page to open the Mail app with an email containing the current URL. You can edit the name of a web clip
  before you save it.

▶ **Return to Safari.** Some links open another application, such as a
  Mailto link opening up the Email app or a Maps link opening the
  Maps app. To return to your web page and Safari, you have to
  press the Home button and then press the Safari icon.

CAUTION: **Consider Surfing Differently on iPad**

Using slow-loading web pages on an iPad can be much more frustrating than on a personal computer because it's not easy to start
doing another task while you are waiting. Also, using the Web might

---

be more fun and satisfying on the iPad than on a personal computer, because you interact with the Web page directly on the iPad, but
waiting for a web page to load may be more frustrating. You may
find that you develop different web-surfing habits on your iPad than
on your personal computer—partly because of the lack of Flash
support, but also because of time constraints.

FIGURE 6.5   Create web clips with Add to Home Screen, and more.

Using Bookmarks

Bookmarks are great time-savers on personal computers. They're even
more important on iPad because of the difficulty of entering URLs as text
and the limitations on screen size.

Follow these instructions to use bookmarks in Safari:

1. To bookmark a web page, with a web page open, press the +
icon. Choose Add Bookmark. Edit the bookmark name, if
desired, and use the drop-down list to place the bookmark in a
folder. (The default is Bookmarks Bar.)

2. To open a bookmark, tap the Bookmarks button, and then press
   Folders to open them and Bookmarks to choose them.

3. To edit a bookmark or folder, tap the Bookmarks button, choose
   a folder or bookmark, and then press Edit. You can then press
   New Folder to create a new folder; press the Delete icon (red cir-
   cle) and choose Delete to delete it; drag the stacks icon to reposi-
   tion the item in its list; and edit the name or folder location by
   pressing the bookmark or folder.

4. To sync bookmarks with Safari on a personal computer, connect
   iPad to your personal computer. In iTunes, select iPad in the sidebar. Click the Info tab, choose Other > Sync Safari bookmarks,
   and then click Apply.

Changing Settings

Safari has a moderate number of settings you can use to control its operation, as follows (see Figure 6.6):

▶ **Search Engine.** Choose Google or Yahoo!.

▶ **Autofill.** Choose this setting to use information from Contacts
   and specify which contact is your personal information; also use
   this setting to turn on storage of names and passwords for various
   web pages.

▶ **Always Show Bookmarks Bar.** Slide to turn the display of the
   Bookmarks Bar on or off. This is a useful convenience feature,
   but it takes up precious vertical screen space.

▶ **Fraud Warning.** Slide to turn warnings for potentially fraudulent
   web sites on or off.

▶ **JavaScript.** Slide to turn JavaScript on or off. (I recommend
   leaving JavaScript on, so you get the functionality it provides,
   unless some web sites start crashing or dramatically slowing your
   machine; in this case, try turning JavaScript off.)

▶ **Block Pop-Ups.** Slide to block pop-ups. (I recommend blocking
   them, as many ads are pop-ups, and who needs the distraction?)

FIGURE 6.6 Safari settings can make your iPad web life easier.

▶ **Accept Cookies.** Slide to either accept all cookies (files that contain information about your visit to a site), to accept cookies only from visited web sites, or not to accept any cookies.

▶ **Databases.** With this setting, you can view the storage size of databases associated with web use, such as for Gmail or Google contacts.

▶ **Clear History, Cookies, Cache.** These options are useful for removing history information you'd rather keep private or for trying to solve potential problems with system instability.

▶ **Developer.** Choose and slide to turn on the developer debug console to help you find and fix errors in a web site you're developing.

So, as you use your iPad, you should find a decreasing number of sites that have multimedia content that doesn't work on iPad. However, this will be a work in progress for a long time to come. If the content you want to view is simply not accessible on iPad, you'll have to look for alternative approaches to getting the information you desire—such as visiting the site using a personal computer.

Summary

In this lesson, you learned how to use Apple's Safari web browser to surf the Web from your iPad, including using the iPad in portrait and landscape modes, opening and navigating web pages, zooming and scrolling, using bookmarks, and changing settings. In the next lesson, you'll learn about creating and managing email on your iPad.

LESSON 7

Synching, Sending, and Receiving Email

In this lesson, you will learn how to make your iPad into a highly capable email machine. You'll find out how to access and synchronize multiple accounts, read and reply to messages, and create and send new messages. Additionally, you'll find out how to configure settings that manage how email works on your iPad.

Setting Up Email Accounts

One of the most promising uses for the iPad is as a quick and easy-to-use email machine. You can use it for occasional keeping up, with a personal computer as your main email platform; in partnership with email on a smartphone such as the iPhone; or as your main email device. You can use a single email account; multiple accounts from Webmail, organizational, and other sources; and separate mail apps such as Gmail. Either way, using email with iPad is flexible and fast.

The iPad directly supports MobileMe and Microsoft Exchange. For setting up access to a Microsoft Exchange account in an organizational setting, you should get help from your organization, because there are specific details for your organization's Exchange setup that you can only get from the people who manage it.

You have the ability to set up multiple email accounts on your iPad. You can then switch among them in the Email app. iPad can be a focal point for all your email, or whatever subset of your email you choose. However, only one account—MobileMe or Microsoft Exchange—can be your main resource for email, calendar, and contacts.

TIP: **Using a Google Account on iPad**

If you have a Google account, set it up as a Microsoft Exchange account to use it as your main resource for email, calendar, and contacts. For information on setting up a Google account as your main account on your iPad, visit: http://www.google.com/support/mobile/bin/answer.py?hl=en&answer=138740.

Make sure you have an active Internet connection. Then follow these steps to set up an account on iPad:

1. Choose Settings > Mail, Contacts, Calendars.

2. Tap Add Account....

3. Choose an account type: Microsoft Exchange, MobileMe, Gmail, Yahoo! Mail, AOL, or Other.

   MobileMe provides specific features for your iPad and can be synchronized with other devices, such as an iPhone, Mac, or PC. Consider trying MobileMe, especially if you don't already have a central source for calendar and contacts to use with your iPad. For more information, visit www.apple.com/mobileme, shown in Figure 7.1.

4. Enter your account information and tap Save.

   In the event that you are lacking information needed for some of the fields, you can contact the service provider for your account or a help desk associate for your account, or you could access the Help files online.

   Your iPad verifies your account information.

5. For a MobileMe account only, select the items you want to use on iPad: Mail, Contacts, Calendars, and Bookmarks.

FIGURE 7.1 MobileMe can keep you synched up.

For MobileMe accounts, you can use the Find My iPad feature to help find your iPad if you lose it or it's stolen. You can also remotely lock or erase the information on your lost or stolen iPad. To enable this, turn on Push for Fetch New Data in Settings for Mail, Contacts, Calendars.

6. For a Microsoft Exchange account only, select the items you want to use on iPad: Mail, Contacts, and Calendars.

For Microsoft Exchange accounts, you can set the number of days of email to synchronize and which folders to push. For instance, you can push your entire Inbox, or just specific folders.

You can set up a special folder on your Microsoft Exchange account and use various rules to only send some email, such as email from certain people that is more likely to be urgent, to that folder. You can then push only that folder to your iPad.

NOTE: **What "Push" Means for Email**

When discussing email, the term "push" refers to the ability of the email host to send, or "push," new emails to your iPad as soon as they're available. Push means you get your email quicker—you don't have to wait for a periodic synchronization request to be issued by your iPad.

If you have multiple accounts, specify which account will be used as your default account for sending mail. This can be done in Settings, as described later in this lesson.

TIP: **Google Accounts Sync Online**

You don't have to use iTunes to sync email, calendar, and/or contacts information from your Google account to your iPad; instead, information is synched over the Internet.

Reading Email

The Mail icon shows the number of unanswered emails in your Inbox from all accounts.

Follow these steps to check your mail:

1. Tap the Mail icon.

2. To change accounts, tap Inbox and then Accounts. Choose an account from the list.

    If the account's Inbox has not been updated by push email or by fetching, it will now update, if you have an active Internet connection.

3. Tap a folder—usually the Inbox, but you can choose other folders as well—to view the email messages in it.

4. To see more messages, scroll to the bottom of the list, and tap Load More Messages.

If you have an active Internet connection, additional messages will load.

5. To delete an email in the message list, swipe left and right over it to see the Delete button, as shown in Figure 7.2. Tap the Delete button to delete the message. To delete multiple messages, tap Edit, select the messages to be deleted, and then tap Delete. (Or, to move messages, start by selecting the messages to move, and then tap Move. Select a mailbox or folder to move the messages to.)

FIGURE 7.2   iPad Mail can display PDFs and many other types of files as attachments.

6. Tap a message description to read the message in full and act on it.

7. To better view the message, use gestures, as with Safari in the previous lesson: Double-tap part of the message once to zoom into it and again to zoom out; pinch to zoom; tap links to follow them; press and hold a link to see its destination address.

8. To view an attachment, tap it.

If you have an active Internet connection, the file downloads and, if the file type is supported by iPad, it displays, as shown in Figure 7.3. To save an image to your Photos album, tap it, and then choose Save Image. For other types of files, if you have an app that can open and potentially edit them, iPad displays a button allowing you to do so. To clear the document from the screen, tap on the screen; then choose Done.

FIGURE 7.3   iPad Mail can display PDFs and many other types of files as attachments.

9. To act on the message, tap an icon to put it in a folder, to delete it, or to reply to it. (When you choose Reply, you also get the option to Reply All or to Forward the message.)

NOTE: **How to Search Email**

To search email, scroll to the top of your mailbox, or tap the Status bar to move quickly to the top. Enter text in the Search field. Tap the fields you want to search. Begin the search—mail already downloaded for the currently open account will be searched. If available, tap "Continue Search on Server" to also search emails stored on the server for your account.

---

10. To view the sender and other recipients of a message, and to have additional options, tap the link, Details, at the top of the email message.

11. Tap on a name to view details; the details then appear, as shown in Figure 7.4. Tap the name to email the person; tap Create New Contact or Add to Existing Contact to add the person's information to your Contacts.

12. Tap Mark as Unread to mark the message as unread and prompt yourself to open it again, whether on iPad or some other system. Tap Hide to hide the details.

NOTE: **How Attachment File Types Work**

For attachments, file types that iPad can display include pictures (JPEG, GIF, and TIFF), which are shown embedded; audio files (MP3, Apple's AAC, WAV, and AIFF), which are played on request; and various kinds of office documents, including PDFs, web pages, plain text files, the iPad's own Pages, Keynote, and Numbers, and Microsoft's Word, Excel, and PowerPoint. Office documents are only viewable, not editable, unless you have specific software to do so. You should be able to select, copy, and paste text out of them, though.

FIGURE 7.4   View another party's details and email them.

Creating and Sending Email

Sending email is easy, especially if you have contact information set up, making email addresses of your correspondents easily available to you. You have a lot of options. Follow these steps:

1. Tap the Compose icon.

2. In the To field, begin to type a name, or tap + to search for a name in your Contacts. Repeat for additional contacts.

If you type in the To field, matching names appear from email addresses you've used before and from your contacts. If you choose contacts, you can use search to hone in on a contact quickly. Both the To field and your contacts search as you type,

so you may only need to type a couple of characters to get the
email address you need, if it's one you've used before.

3. To add to the Cc: or Bcc: fields, or to change the From: address,
tap the line showing them to open it. Enter the additional email
addresses, as shown in Figure 7.5. To change the From: address,
tap the current address, and choose which of your email accounts
to use from the list that appears.

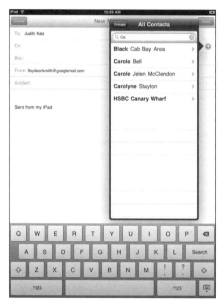

FIGURE 7.5   Pick a contact to send to.

4. Enter a subject and type your message.

While entering a message, to save a draft, tap Cancel, and then
tap Save. You can recover the message from the Drafts mailbox.

5. Tap Send. This completes the process and sends your message.

Changing Mail Settings

Some email settings are set in the mail application or when configuring the account, as described earlier in this lesson. There are also a number of settings you can use to manage the display and functionality of all email inboxes that you access through the iPad Email app, as shown in Figure 7.6:

▶ **Accounts.** This setting enables you to add, delete, and configure accounts.

▶ **Fetch New Data.** For accounts that do not push email, the Email app will fetch it. Choose a schedule for fetching. (Fetching less frequently saves battery life.)

▶ **Show Messages Number.** This setting enables you to specify how many recent messages to show without having to tap a button to load more messages.

FIGURE 7.6   Mail settings bring your iPad email to life.

▶ **Preview Lines, Font Size.** With this setting, you can specify the number of preview lines and the font size used in displaying the message list.

▶ **Show To/Cc Label, Ask Before Deleting, Load Remote Images.** You can turn these options on and off to control how iPad works with individual emails.

> NOTE: **Fetching Instead of Pushing**
>
> If your email account doesn't push new emails out to you as they come in, your account can request them periodically. This is called fetching.

▶ **Always Bcc Myself.** Turning on this setting will help you manage the emails you send or forward by always sending a blind carbon copy to yourself.

▶ **Signature.** With this setting, you can enter text to append to the bottom of each email, such as your name, email address, and phone number.

▶ **Default Account.** If you have multiple email accounts, you can specify which one to use for sending emails from other apps, such as the Notes app described in Lesson 8.

▶ **Contacts Sort.** Here you can specify the default sort order and display order for contacts.

▶ **Calendars.** This setting enables you to specify whether new invitations generate an alert, how far back to synchronize events, and which time zone to use for managing your events. (You should change the time zone when you travel.)

Summary

In this lesson, you learned how to set up email accounts on the iPad; how to read, create, and send email; and how to change email settings. In the next lesson you learn how to use contacts, a key type of data for tying your personal organizational impact together, and notes.

LESSON 8

Using Contacts and Notes

In this lesson, you will learn how to use your iPad Contacts and Notes, and which apps will help you stay organized and in touch.

Setting Up Contacts

Keeping track of one's contacts has always been an effort. Millions of blank contacts books, Rolodexes for business cards, and other devices have been sold just for this purpose. Today, with more ways to reach people than ever, contacts information is even more important.

The iPad is a great device for working with contacts. The large screen, easy portability, and ease of use help to make it ideal for capturing and exchanging information. It's easy to look things up on iPad to fill out contact information. Once you've entered the contact information, it's also easy to email people (see the previous lesson), pull up a number to call them, or integrate an address into a note. To add a great deal more power, the iPad makes it easy to share contact information with your other devices.

> **TIP: Faces "Make" Facebook**
>
> There are many reasons why Facebook is one of the most popular online services around, but one of them has to be simply the sheer power of "putting a face to a name" online. Similarly, it's surprising how much using photos on your contacts information brings them to life. When you set out to contact someone using their photo,

you're using the more social side of your brain, recognizing faces rather than reading words. Try to find time to associate photos with all your contacts; it makes picking people out for sending emails or setting up meetings a real joy.

Creating or Updating a Contact

Even if you get contacts onto your iPad by synchronizing them, there will still be occasion to enter contacts directly onto your iPad. Also, a quick look at the process makes you more aware of just what the potential fields are, helping you do a better job of capturing relevant information and synching what you capture across platforms.

TIP: **Get Information Together First**

Because the iPad offers limited multitasking, it's often helpful to try to handle sub-tasks (such as getting a photo for someone) before starting the overall task (such as creating a new contact for that person). Try to have contact information (such as email addresses, address information, and so on) at hand, and have a photo ready in the Photo app (see Lesson 11, "Getting Apps from the App Store"), before creating or modifying a contact, or you may have to start over—perhaps even several times. Consider consolidating the relevant information in a note, as described at the end of this lesson, pasting it into the Notes field of a contact, and then cutting and pasting each part of it into the appropriate field of a note.

Follow these steps to create a new contact:

1. Consider which photo you want to use for the person, business, and so on and bring that photo into an easy-to-find place in your Photo Album.

TIP: **Use Photos and Screenshots, Too**

In place of a photo for a business contact, consider using a screen-shot of their business from Street View in the Maps app. You can do the same for teachers (use their school) and friends (use their house). For real photos of people, Facebook is a good source. See

Lesson 10 for working with Maps and Lesson 12 for working with photos and other images, including screenshots.

2. Press the Contacts app to start it.

Figure 8.1 shows a completed contact for reference.

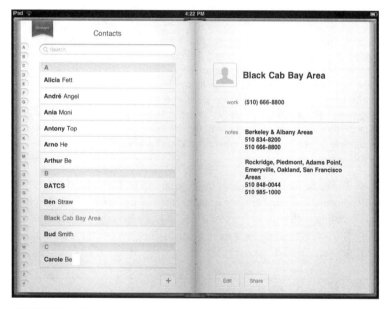

FIGURE 8.1 Make your Contacts as complete as possible.

3. Press the + button to add a contact.

4. Press Add Photo to add a photo.

A list of photo albums appears.

5. Pick out the photo you want by pressing it.

The photo will be added to the contact.

6. Enter the first name, last name, and/or company name for the contact.

7. Specify the type of phone number. If the default (mobile) is correct, there's no need to change it. However, if it's a different type of phone number, click the word "mobile." A list of alternatives will appear, including mobile, home, work, home fax, work fax, pager, assistant, car, company main, and radio. Choose the most appropriate descriptor.

CAUTION: **Consider Editing Contacts Elsewhere**

At this writing, iPad does not seem to offer any way to add an additional phone number to a contact besides the one that's present by default (or, potentially, several, if the contact was created on another platform). For additional phone numbers, you'll have to either put the additional information in the Notes field; create a separate, additional contact for the same person with a different phone number—which can make it quicker to reach a given phone number; or update the contact on another platform, such as a personal computer, and then sync the contact back to the iPad.

---

8. Enter the phone number of the type specified. If you need to add a pause to a number—for instance, for dialing an extension, or dialing with a phone card or discount number—add a comma. For a longer pause, add more commas. Test the result for accuracy on your smartphone.

NOTE: **Use Country Codes**

For overseas phone numbers, include the country code, preceded by the + symbol. If you might be calling a U.S.-based number when you're traveling outside the country, consider starting the number with +1, followed by the area code. The number will then work from overseas without any fiddling around.

---

9. Enter the email address.

10. Enter the URL of the person's home page, if any.

   This can be the URL of someone's Facebook page, LinkedIn profile, and so forth.

11. To specify the type of address, press the address type—the default is "home"—and choose the appropriate label: Home, Work, or Other. Then enter the address, if any.

Enter the street address, city, state, and ZIP code. If the country isn't the U.S., press the country name and then choose the correct country from the scrolling list that appears.

NOTE: **Enter Full International Addresses**

U.S.-style addresses are quite simple compared to some other countries, which tend to include house names, street names, county names, and so on. If a mailing address is too complex to simplify into the Contacts address block, consider entering it into the Notes field.

---

12. If desired, enter Notes—this can be any information you want to remember about the person.

13. To add more information, click the + next to Add field. Then choose a field from the list, as shown in Figure 8.2. Fields

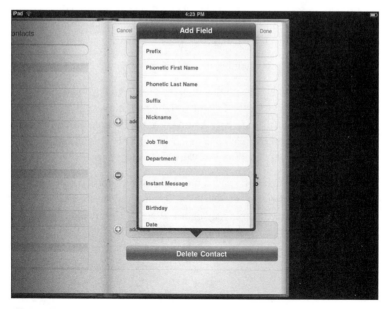

FIGURE 8.2 Additional fields can be added to your contacts.

available include Prefix (such as Mr., Mrs., Miss, and so on), Phonetic First Name or Phonetic Last Name, Middle Name, Suffix (such as Esq. for an attorney), Nickname, Job Title, Department, Instant Message address, Birthday date, and Date (intended to be used for remembering an anniversary or similar type of date).

Searching and Updating Contacts

When searching for contacts, you can only search by first name, last name, or company name. However, you'll find that sometimes you'll enter a search string, such as "An," and have contact names appear that don't begin with "An."

The reason you see additional contacts in the search results is that the search includes the company name associated with the contact. However, the company name is not displayed in search results if there is also a person's name, which leads to your getting some search results that don't visibly match your search string.

For instance, a search for "An" will bring up people named "Andy," but also people of any name who work for "An Enormous Company"—but not people who work for "A Rich and Enormous Company."

Use these tips to help you with searching in contacts:

▶ When you use the search function, the on-screen keyboard automatically capitalizes the first letter. Using an initial capital letter means that matches are only returned for the beginning of a word within a first name, last name, or company name. For instance, searching for "Tr" will return "Trish" but not "Patricia."

▶ To broaden the search results, turn off caps lock for the initial letter. You will then get matches from within words in the first name, last name, or company name, as well as from the beginning of the words. Searching for "tr" will return both "Trish" and "Patricia," as shown in Figure 8.3.

FIGURE 8.3   Searching with all lowercase letters matches within words.

▶ For Exchange accounts only, to search an enterprise Global Address List (GAL), tap Groups and then the Exchange server name. Although search will work, you will not have the ability to edit contacts you find, nor will you be able to save them to the iPad.

▶ Also for Exchange accounts only, to search a Lightweight Directory Access Protocol (LDAP) server, tap Groups and then the LDAP server name. As mentioned in the previous search option, although you can search for a contact, you won't be able to edit them or save them to the iPad.

Syncing Contacts

You can bring in contacts from other platforms, and share the contact information that you create or edit on iPad in several ways:

▶ Use a MobileMe, Microsoft Exchange, or other host as your main source for email, calendar, and/or contacts information (see the previous lesson).

▶ Use iTunes to sync contacts from Google, Yahoo!, or with applications on your computer (see Lesson 10, "Working with Maps").

▶ Have your organization help you access internal contacts directories by setting up an Exchange account with contacts enabled, or an LDAP account. Access to such accounts is read-only; you can't edit contacts you access from Exchange or LDAP, nor can you save these contacts to your iPad.

Creating and Sharing Notes

The Notes app may just be one of the best uses of the iPad as a kind of super-powered version of a paper notebook. Compared to a paper notebook, using the Notes app on iPad has many advantages, as follows:

▶ **More flexible.** In addition to Notes, there are other apps available to you on the iPad, and with a Wi-Fi iPad, you can connect to the Internet in many places where you might be taking notes; with an iPad Wi-Fi+3G, you can connect to the Internet from nearly anywhere.

▶ **Searchable.** You can search the titles of notes on iPad, and the entire contents of notes when sent as email or incorporated in other iPad apps (such as the Pages app available on iPad) or applications on a personal computer.

▶ **Sharable.** You can easily email notes, which makes them great for sharing the proceedings of meetings and so on, and sync them with some email applications, such as Microsoft Outlook (see Lesson 16, "Using iTunes to Sync Multimedia and More").

The Notes app has two main features: the list of notes, and individual notes. In the next two sections, I show you how to create an individual note and then all the things you can do with a note once you've created it.

Creating a Note

Follow these steps to create a Note:

1. Press the Notes app to start it.

2. Press the + button to create a note.

3. Enter the name of the note on the first line. Only about 20 characters will reliably display in the list of notes that you've written. (The number of characters displayed fluctuates, depending on the day or date that the iPad displays next to the note name, as well as on word breaks and the width of specific characters.)

4. Type the note. The note that appears will be similar to the one shown in Figure 8.4. Typing speed and ease are very important in note taking. One helpful feature is to end each sentence with two spaces; the iPad will insert a full stop and a single space, then start the next sentence with a single capital letter.

TIP: **Save Keystrokes on Punctuation**

The only punctuation characters available on the initial iPad onscreen keyboard are the comma, full stop, and (with shifting) the exclamation point and question mark. Consider using a kind of punctuation shorthand, such as lots of ellipses (...) instead of dashes, and spelling out numbers instead of using digits, to speed typing.

---

5. Press the keyboard key on the onscreen keyboard to make the onscreen keyboard go away so you can examine the note more easily.

6. You can edit the note at any time, and at any point. Press anywhere on the note to place the insertion point there, and to bring up the onscreen keyboard. Make your changes as needed.

FIGURE 8.4   Use notes to record events, your thoughts, and more.

TIP: **Abbreviate Names to Fit**

Only the first 20 characters or so of the note's name will be visible in the list of notes, so consider using some kind of abbreviated naming convention for your notes. I start most of my notes with the date of creation, a short description of the place (such as "CCC" for the Commonwealth Club of California), and then a distinguishing word or two about the event or meeting.

Emailing and Managing Notes

One of the great advantages of using your iPad for taking notes, instead of a pen and paper, is being able to email them. You can also store many more notes on your iPad than you can in a paper notebook.

Tips for using notes include:

▶ **To email a note**, simply press the email symbol at the bottom of a note to email it, as shown in Figure 8.5. You can email it to anyone interested, or only email it to yourself, for forwarding from the Mail app on your iPad or from an email application or service on a personal computer.

FIGURE 8.5 Email your notes to anyone interested in them.

▶ **To see note names,** press the Notes button. In Portrait mode, the list of names of notes is hidden.

▶ **To read through notes**, use the arrow keys to move through notes, or press on note titles in the list of notes to move among them.

▶ **To search notes**, turn your iPad horizontally, if it isn't already, so the Search field shows up. Enter characters one at a time to build up your search string. As you enter each character, iPad will display the list of notes that include the string of all the characters you've entered.

▶ **To delete a note,** scroll to the bottom of the note and press the trash can to delete the note. (It's not necessary to delete notes to try to free up a large amount of storage capacity on your iPad; notes are quite small. A gigabyte of storage holds about one million notes.)

▶ **To manage your notes by date,** be aware of the following information. Notes are listed by the date of last modification. If you
want to store the date on which your note was created, you have
to include it in the note itself. (It might be helpful to put the date
of creation in the titles of your notes, so you still have a record of
the date of the event if you edit the note later.)

▶ **To sync notes,** see Lesson 16, which explains how to sync notes
with certain applications using iTunes.

CAUTION: **Watch Out for Shortened Notes**

The notes you create in the Notes app can be much larger than,
say, the Notes supported by Microsoft Outlook. If you use iTunes to
sync your notes with Microsoft Outlook or another personal information management platform, check carefully to see just how much
information gets through without truncation before counting on this
method of transferring information.

Please note that information is easily lost in the following ways:

▶ **A copy on a target platform.** When you synchronize a long
iPad note with another application that supports shorter notes,
you lose information on the synched copy due to its being truncated on the other platform.

▶ **The iPad-based original.** If you edit a truncated note on another
platform, the truncated note becomes the newer copy. When you
synch the iPad with the other platform, the longer version of the
note you have stored on the iPad is replaced in favor of the
newer version that was first truncated and then edited on the
other platform.

Summary

In this lesson, you learned how to use Contacts and Notes on the iPad. In
the next lesson, you'll learn how to use the Calendar app as a further part
of staying organized.

LESSON 9

Getting the Most Out of the Calendar

In this lesson, you will learn how to update, view, and synchronize your calendar, and receive alerts from it in a timely way to help you get things done.

How the Calendar Helps

Being where you need to be, when you need to be there, is an ongoing challenge for almost all of us. Being so portable, so easy to use, and so well integrated with other apps such as email and maps, the iPad works very well as a personal organizational tool. It also "plays well with others," sharing events and updates with mobile phones and personal computers.

The calendar is a crucial part of staying organized, and a great thing to have with you "on the go." The iPad is particularly well-suited for calendar use because of its large screen, letting you see lots of information at once, and without having to hassle with a laptop.

> **TIP: Synchronize Calendars**
> To sync calendars, use the iPad preferences panel in iTunes (see Lesson 16, "Using iTunes to Sync Multimedia and More"), or turn on Calendars in your iPad Settings for syncing with a Microsoft Exchange or MobileMe account (see Lesson 7, "Synching, Sending, and Receiving Email").

Viewing Your Calendar

Viewing what's on your calendar is a daily activity, and one that's strengthened if you can make changes and additions as needed. The calendar on your iPad has some real strengths in this regard:

▶ **Size and attractiveness.** The large screen size and the attractive appearance of your iPad's display make it great for managing calendar entries compared with, say, a mobile phone.

▶ **Portability.** You can easily take your iPad with you, so you have your calendar entries—and the ability to add to or update them—close at hand.

▶ **Interactivity.** Your iPad displays alerts on the home screen, even when it is otherwise inert, and it is easy to use for updating events and adding new information (see information on adding events later in this lesson).

▶ **Integration.** Your iPad calendar can reflect information stored in other calendars and can be updated by entries made on other platforms (see the Tip about syncing calendars).

CAUTION: **Don't Knock Your iPad**

At this writing, you can't swipe to move to the next or previous page of the calendar. Don't knock your iPad off its stand trying to do so! Instead, use the date timeline at the bottom of the screen to change pages.

Here's how to view your calendar:

1. Tap the Calendar app to start it.

The calendar then appears, as shown in Figure 9.1.

2. If you have multiple calendars set up, tap the Calendars button and then select a calendar. Tap All Calendars to select them all.

FIGURE 9.1 Your calendar shows your events at a glance.

3. Tap buttons on the top of the screen to move among Day, Week, Month, and List views.

   All of the views are useful, and you can switch from portrait to landscape mode to see which one you prefer for each view. The List view, shown in Figure 9.2, is a great combination of a scrollable list of events on the left and an easy-to-use, hour-by-hour view of the current day on the right.

4. Tap buttons on the bottom of the screen to move to a different day, week, or month, depending on the current view.

5. Use the arrow keys to move one day, week, or month at a time.

6. Tap a time period to move to it, or tap on the left or right arrows to slide backward or forward in time. As you tap the arrows, the

FIGURE 9.2   If it's List view, it probably won't be missed.

time period you're currently moving over displays onscreen. The main calendar display doesn't change until you stop dragging. When you move away from the current time period, the time period displayed is highlighted by a white box, whereas the current day, week, or month remains highlighted with a blue highlight.

7. Tap the Today button to return to the current day, week, or month.

TIP: **How to Search Calendar Items**

Searches only apply to the title of an event, the location, and the name(s) of people invited—not to notes and other fields. To search, enter the word or words to search in the Search field; as you enter text, matching events appear in a list below. Click Search to move the keyboard away and view the complete results list.

Creating a Calendar Event

Many of your calendar events may come from entries made on other devices such as a laptop or smartphone. However, you will likely want to enter, update, and, in many cases, share information directly from the iPad as well.

Follow these steps to add a calendar event:

1. Move the calendar to the time period in which you want to make a new entry, to check that the time is available. (Refer to the "Viewing your Calendar" section found earlier in this lesson for details.)

2. Tap the + button in the lower-right corner of the calendar. The Add Event entry area appears, as shown in Figure 9.3.

FIGURE 9.3   Add events to stay up to date.

TIP: **From Email to Calendar**

If you receive event information in text form—for instance, in an email—copy it out of the email and then paste it into the Notes area of a new event. Then you can copy and paste information in the Notes area into the corresponding fields of the event.

3. Enter the event title. The title should have easily recognized key words up front when looking at a shrunken view, as on a mobile phone or in the Month view on iPad.

4. Enter the location of the event. For maximum usability with your iPad's Maps app, or similar apps on other platforms, consider entering only the street address (such as 435 Post St, San Francisco). You can put the building name and other useful address information in the Notes.

   Also consider getting any directions that you need now, and entering them in the Notes area for use on the way to the appointment.

5. Tap the Starts/Ends area to enter the start and end time, or use the All-Day slider to indicate an all-day event.

6. Enter the starting and ending time using the date and time indicators. Unlike some other scheduling tools, you can specify times to the nearest five minutes, not just to the nearest quarter hour or half hour.

   To take travel times into account, you can either lengthen the event to include the travel times, or create separate entries for the journey, or simply remember to account for it by using care when scheduling adjacent calendar events. Consider creating a policy for yourself that fits your needs, such as not noting journey times of ten minutes or less, but creating separate entries for journey times of fifteen minutes or more. Such an approach is particularly useful for potentially complicated or important events, such as traveling to the airport for a trip, or driving to a job interview.

7. Tap Repeat to enter any repetitious information. You can choose to repeat the event every day, week, two weeks, month, or year. Certain more sophisticated choices, such as the last Friday of every month, are not available to be specified in Calendar.

8. Tap Invitees to enter people to invite.

TIP: **Use Calendar Invitations**

Consider making it a habit to invite people to an event using your calendar. That way, they not only are reminded of the event when it's created, but they can be automatically kept up to date with any changes as well.

---

9. Tap Alert to specify when the alert for the event will appear—in 5 minutes, 15 minutes, 30 minutes, 1 hour, 2 hours, 1 day, 2 days, or on the date of the event. (You will get the opportunity to enter a second alert as well.) Use a time period—or time periods, if you use two alerts—that will allow for both travel to the event and preparation for it.

NOTE: **Alerts Appear Everywhere**

When you reach the time specified by the Alert for an event, an alert appears onscreen. Alerts appear even if you are on the Lock screen that appears when you start your iPad.

---

10. Tap Availability to show how the event appears in your calendar—busy, free, tentative, or out of office. This kind of busy/free notification is particularly useful if others are using your calendar to create events for you, or including you.

11. Tap Notes to enter notes about the event. Use the Notes section to organize and store related information about the event.

12. Tap Done to record the event. The event will then appear in your Calendar.

TIP: **Use the Calendar for To-Dos**

The Calendar app can be used as a to-do list. You can create all-day events or time-specific events. Alternatively, you might consider using one of the many To Do list manager apps available in the App Store.

CAUTION: **Watch Out for Time Zones**

The iPad does not necessarily update the time for you when you are traveling through different time zones. Use the Date & Time settings (see Lesson 5, "Customizing General Settings for Your iPad") to update the time when you travel.

Responding to Meeting Invitations

You can only receive meeting invitations if you have a Microsoft Exchange account on your iPad with Calendars enabled (see Lesson 7, "Synching, Sending, and Receiving Email"). If you receive an invitation, follow these steps:

1. Find the meeting invitation in the calendar, or the event notification in the In tray icon in the corner of your screen. The meeting invitation looks very similar to a new meeting, as shown in Figure 9.3 above.

2. To view contact information for the meeting organizer, tap "Invitation From." Tap the email address to send the organizer an email message.

3. To view contact information for invitees, tap "Invitees." Tap an invitee's name to see their contact information. Tap the email address to send the invitee an email message.

4. To set an alert, tap Alert and specify the alert time.

5. To add a comment, tap Add Comments and enter your comments.

Comments appear in the Info screen for the meeting and may be visible to all participants.

6. To respond to the invitation, tap Accept, Maybe, or Decline. Add comments for the meeting organizer if desired, then tap Done.

NOTE: **More Email Help**

You may receive meeting invitations by email instead of in your calendar. Open the email message and respond as indicated to accept or decline the invitation.

Subscribing to Calendars

Subscribing to a calendar allows calendar events from other calendars to appear on yours. You can't edit the entries or create new events for those calendars.

You can subscribe to a wide range of calendars, including Yahoo!, Google, and Macintosh iCal calendars. Any calendar that uses the CalDAV or iCalendar, or .ics, format will work. (Yahoo!, Google, and iCal calendars support both.)

The iPad accepts invitations from iCalendar accounts, but not CalDAV accounts.

Follow these instructions to subscribe to a calendar:

1. Tap the Settings application icon.

2. Choose Mail, and then Contacts. Tap Calendar.

3. Tap Add Account, and then choose Other.

4. Choose Add Subscribed Calendar, for an iCalendar account, or Add CalDAV account.

5. Enter the account information.

6. Tap Next to verify the account.

7. Tap Save.

Summary

In this lesson, you learned how to view your calendar, create events, subscribe to calendars, and respond to meeting invitations. In the next lesson, I'll introduce working with the Maps app.

LESSON 10

Working with Maps

In this lesson, you learn how to use the Maps app to find your current location and how to use the built-in compass and Street View. You also learn how to navigate different map views, use the Traffic overlay, get directions, and more.

Getting the Most Out of Maps

Mapping is one of the most exciting apps on your iPad. It does have a few potentially frustrating pitfalls, but less so if you are aware and can watch out for them.

Here are a few iPad and digital mapping basics to help you get the most out of maps:

▶ Your current location is calculated using data from Wi-Fi sources and, if you have a Wi-Fi+3G iPad, cellphone towers. You must be online to use Maps.

▶ Wi-Fi source information may not be very accurate for hotspots that cover a large area, and GPS, for those who have a Wi-Fi+3G iPad, is sometimes inaccurate. As a result, your current location information may not be fully accurate. For best results, enter your starting point's address directly into the Maps app if needed; then follow the instructions carefully to stay on track, even if you have 3G and a live Internet connection throughout the trip.

▶ Online maps are constructed from a wide range of different data sources with varying degrees of age and accuracy. Don't be too surprised if you're told to drive the wrong way on a one-way street, or to take a long walk on a short pier, or to cross an international border to visit the drugstore—and be sure not to do it!

▶ Traffic information on digital maps is spotty; and many of the things you really want to know—such as how long a traffic jam will last—can't be answered by a computer.

There are many great things about using the iPad for mapping. Let's look at some of the benefits:

▶ **It's functional when on the move.** There's a lot of functionality for free with a live Internet connection (you'll need 3G when you're on the move). Finding your location, getting turn-by-turn directions, and adding support for geographically aware social networking are all at your fingertips.

▶ **It's functional at a Wi-Fi hotspot.** There's still a lot you can do when you're not on the move if you have a live Internet connection. You can look at maps, use Street View, get and save directions, and get local business information.

▶ **It's easy to use.** The size and direct tactile input of the iPad are very well suited for use with online mapping, and the maps displayed look spectacular.

Follow the instructions in this lesson to get the most out of your mapping experience on iPad.

Searching for and Viewing Locations

Mapping is all about locations, of course. You can use your iPad to search for locations, mark them, and view them in several modes, including in Street View.

Finding Your Current Location and Showing the Compass

For mapping and directions, it's very important to see where you are—or, at least, where the Maps app thinks you are! Follow these instructions to find yourself on the map:

1. Tap the Maps app to open and start it.

2. Tap the compass icon in the Maps app's status bar at the top of the screen. This re-centers the map on your current location, which is shown by a blue dot.

3. To get information about your current location, tap the blue dot. A brief description of your current location appears.

4. To see a fuller description of your current location, press the "i" in the brief description. A fuller description of your current location displays, with options, as shown in Figure 10.1. These

FIGURE 10.1 The Maps app gives you many options for each location.

options are described in the section "Finding Directions and Businesses."

5. To see your current location in Street View, press the Street View icon. Your location appears as described in the following section.

6. To show a digital compass, press the compass icon again. The map updates to show a compass icon and the direction of North, as shown in Figure 10.2 (shown in Terrain view, described later in this lesson). Hold the iPad flat to see which way the compass is facing and find North. Text labels appear sideways unless you point the iPad in a northerly direction.

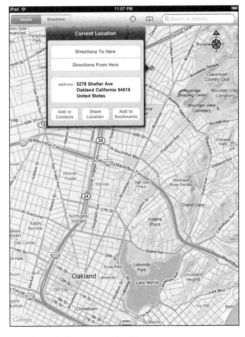

FIGURE 10.2   Let Google Maps on iPad be your compass.

7. To return to map view, without the compass, press the compass icon again.

Using Street View

Street View is an amazing capability of Google Maps. Using Street View, you can navigate onscreen as if you were live and in person in places all over the world.

Google sent specially equipped cars and trucks around the streets and highways of most countries in the world to capture images, and then stitched them together to create panoramas of a large part of the world, as seen from its roads.

> NOTE: **Use Street View for a Preview**
>
> Street View can be a wonderful tool to help orient yourself to a destination you're traveling to. "Experiencing" the destination in Street View gives you a helpful tour of a new area, making it easier to find your way around.

The only thing more amazing than Street View itself is Street View as seen and used on the iPad. The large and bright screen, the fact that the iPad is handheld, the way in which you can take it with you to get directions, and the way you manipulate the screen directly with your hands, bring Street View to a new level.

Follow these steps to use Street View:

1. Bring up a description of a location, as described in the previous section.

2. Press the Street View icon to see the location in Street View.

The location appears in Street View, as shown in Figure 10.3.

FIGURE 10.3   Street View immerses you in an onscreen "real world."

   3. From Street View, use gestures to look around within the view. Drag the image to pan in all directions.

NOTE: **No Street View Zoom**

You can't zoom in while in Street View, as you can on some other platforms for Google Maps, because Google Maps is already using all the information it has to show the full-screen pictures you're seeing.

---

   4. To change your location within Street View, press the arrows located on the road (where available). Your viewpoint will move down the road in the indicated direction. You can then pan in all directions again.

   5. To exit Street View, press the map icon in the lower-right corner.

Using Map Views and Traffic

Google Maps defaults to what's called the Classic view. This is a map view, with lots of useful detail, such as lot outlines for homes, businesses, and so on, for many locations.

To see additional views, put your finger in the lower-right corner, where it appears as if the map is curled away from the corner. Drag the corner up and to the left. You'll uncover mapping options, as shown in Figure 10.4.

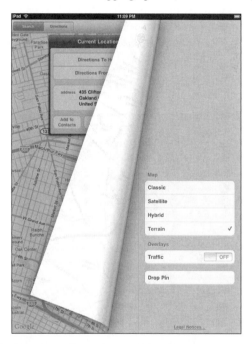

FIGURE 10.4   Mapping options give you lots of power.

Not all options are available for all locations. Where available, the mapping options are as follows:

▶ **Classic.** The default view that shows lot outlines, businesses, and other useful features.

▶ **Satellite.** A view made up of satellite photographs taken during the daytime on non-cloudy days. Shows an amazing level of detail.

▶ **Hybrid.** A very useful view for familiarizing yourself with an area (or just for gawking around in your current area). Combines text showing street names, business names, icons for things like transit stops, and satellite photography.

▶ **Terrain.** A map showing elevations, street names, and major feature names, such as parks and university campuses. Great for planning a walk, a bicycle ride, or a hike.

▶ **Traffic.** An overlay that shows traffic conditions on major streets, highways, and freeways, shown overlaying the Terrain map on Figure 10.5. Green shows roads operating at or near top posted speed—or, for highways and freeways, more than 50 mph; yellow is slower than the posted speed—or, for highways and freeways, from 25–50 mph; and red is below 25 mph.

FIGURE 10.5   Traffic information can overlay any view, including the Satellite view.

▶ **Drop pin.** Puts a pin into the map that you can use to get information on that location. You can also drop a pin by pressing and holding on the map directly.

Finding Destinations and Businesses

Finding locations is easy on iPad, though entering addresses using the onscreen keyboard can be a bit tricky. It might take a couple of tries.

Once you find a location, you can view it (including in Street View, where available) and drop a pin on locations of your own.

Follow these steps to search for a location:

1. Press the Search button in the upper-right corner. The map you've viewed most recently in Search appears.

2. Press the Search field. Press the X to clear it, if needed. The onscreen keyboard appears, along with a list of recent searches.

3. Type an address or other search information. Google is pretty good with relatively free-form searches, but the most reliable format is still the street address (number and street name) followed by the city, or an abbreviation ("sf" or "nyc", for instance).

You can also try more general searches, such as "picante berk" for a Mexican food restaurant in Berkeley, California, but be careful of multiple matches and mismatches. You might end up being steered to the Berkshires in Massachusetts!

4. Press Search on the keyboard. One or more pins appear to show matches for your search.

5. Use gestures such as pinching to zoom, and panning to look at different areas of the map, to focus in on the pin(s). If there are multiple pins, tap a pin to see the descriptor for it.

6. The destination becomes a Recent, meaning it appears in the Recents list for searches and for creating directions.

7. Tap the blue "i" on a descriptor to see detailed information about a location. Detailed information about the location appears, as described earlier in this lesson.

8. Press one of the buttons in the information to get directions to the destination or directions from the destination to somewhere else, to add the destination to your Contacts, to share the destination via email (this doesn't close the Maps app), or to add the location to your Bookmarks. Press the URL, if one is provided, to go to the associated web page (this does close the Maps app). Press the Street View icon to see the location in Street View, as described earlier in this lesson.

> **NOTE: Directions and Bookmarks**
>
> For information about getting directions, or about using Maps Bookmarks, see the relevant sections later in this lesson.

Sharing the destination via email gives you a chance to add a note, and then send both a Microsoft Outlook business card file and a Google Maps link to the destination.

9. To drop a pin on a location, simply zoom in very tightly (down to the level where you can see lot lines, where available); then press on the map in the desired spot. A pin appears, showing the destination address.

10. To see and use options for the dropped pin's location, press the blue "i" button. Options appear, as shown previously in Figure 10.4 and described in Step 7.

11. To remove the pin, press the Remove Pin button in the information area.

> **CAUTION: Watch Out for "Big" Destinations**
>
> It's easy to get "bad" locations and directions for some destinations. Many hospitals and restaurants, among others, have several

locations. Universities, national parks, and other extensive destinations often have multiple entrances or addresses, some of which may be miles from where you actually want to go, such as the entrance to a national park or the main parking lot. Double-check that you're being pointed to the right destination; you may need to check a web site or call to be sure.

Getting Directions and Using Bookmarks

Getting directions, and helping you follow them, is one of the most useful things a portable device can do. With iPad, directions are uniquely functional, due to the size of the display and the way you manipulate the screen directly.

Follow these steps to view directions:

1. To make entering directions easier, first find the start and end points onscreen (if neither of them is your current location, or already a Recent), as described in the previous section. The start or end point will now appear in the Recents list for searches, making it easy to select for directions.

2. To make a point a Bookmark, touch its pin to open the information area for it, as described in the previous section. Press Add to Bookmarks; the Add Bookmark window will open. Edit the name, using the onscreen keyboard, and press Save.

3. To begin getting directions, press the Directions button in the upper right. Or, from a location description or a Bookmark (press the Bookmarks icon), press the Directions To Here button or the Directions From Here button. The Start-End area appears in the upper right corner of the screen. The Start and/or End areas may be filled in with Current Location or a spot that you specified.

4. To enter or change the Start location, press in the first area. A list of Recents appears, and the onscreen keyboard appears as well, as shown in Figure 10.6.

FIGURE 10.6   Recents and Bookmarks help you generate directions quickly and easily.

5. Press a Recent to choose it, or enter an address using the onscreen keyboard, as described in the previous section.

6. Enter the End location—press in the Destination area to search, use a Recent, or use a Bookmark, as described in the previous steps. The End location appears onscreen, as does a strip to select Driving, Transit, or Walking directions.

7. Choose Driving, Transit, or Walking. For Transit, press the Time button and then press Depart to enter the time of departure or arrival, as shown in Figure 10.7.

8. Press Start to view the directions. The directions appear in the strip at the bottom of the screen.

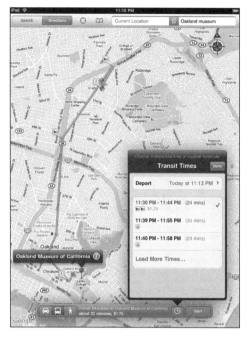

FIGURE 10.7   You can select Driving, Transit (with times), or Walking directions, and view estimated travel time, distance, and/or cost for each.

9. To see step-by-step directions, press the arrow keys at the bottom of the screen. To see complete directions, press the list icon; the list of steps appears onscreen, as shown in Figure 10.8.

You can pinch to zoom and drag the map "underneath" the list, or turn the iPad to portrait or landscape mode, without disturbing the directions list or changing its relative location, to get the most useful information onscreen at once.

TIP: **Photos Can Help with Maps**

If you have a Wi-Fi-only iPad, or if you have a Wi-Fi+3G iPad but think you might lose cellular data coverage, you can still use iPad maps and directions (though not with turn-by-turn support). Simply create the directions and get the list to display on top of the relative map before you set out, while you still have coverage. Get the Maps screen arranged in the most helpful manner you can. Then capture the screen by holding down the Home button and briefly pressing the Power button. The captured image will appear in Photos, and you can view it there as needed during your trip.

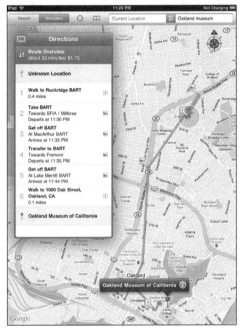

FIGURE 10.8   This directions list shows walking, Bay Area Rapid Transit (BART) stops, and costs.

Summary

In this lesson, you learned how to use the Maps app to find your current location, get directions, use Street View and other views, get traffic updates, and more. In the next lesson, I'll show you how to get the most out of the App Store in getting apps for your iPad.

LESSON 11

Getting Apps from the App Store

In this lesson, you learn about apps: how to find, purchase (if necessary), and download them from the App Store on iPad. You also learn how to rate, report problems with, and update apps.

Understanding the App Store's Success

The Apple App Store for the iPod Touch, iPhone, and now iPad is an amazing modern success story, and one of the most important reasons that the iPad has gotten off to a great start as a new product.

The original idea for the iPhone was that the only add-on software for it would be in the form of custom web pages written in the emerging technology, HTML 5. This is good to understand, because Web pages are still an important tool for delivering software functionality on the iPhone and the iPad today.

The App Store was developed because developers asked Apple for a way to create apps like the ones Apple put on the iPod and iPhone. Apple obliged, and the App Store has become an unexpected success.

Aside from the size of their screens, the iPad is not much different than the iPhone. However, the iPad's larger screen is an important difference because, with five times more space, more relevant information is available onscreen at once, making many tasks easier to complete. Also, the iPad inherits the App Store infrastructure, adding a bit of complexity to it.

There are now three major kinds of apps, as follows:

- ▶ **iPad-specific apps.** One bundle of software that only works on iPad.

- ▶ **Universal apps.** A bundle of software with an extra chunk of software code and two sets of graphics: one for iPad and one for iPhone. The app runs in full resolution on either platform.

- ▶ **iPhone-specific apps.** These apps are made to run on iPhone and have iPhone-sized graphics.

There's no real problem with using iPhone-specific apps on the iPad. You download and run them just like a universal app, or an iPad-specific app. The only difference is that, when you run an iPhone-specific app on the iPad, it appears small compared to iPad apps, albeit very crisp-looking.

If you want, you can expand the app to nearly full-screen by pushing the 2x button. This makes it bigger, and easier to touch the right points on it, but makes the graphics look a bit rough and unfinished, as shown in Figure 11.1.

FIGURE 11.1   iPhone-specific apps work fine on iPad.

To return to small-but-crisp mode, push the 1x button, and the image shrinks down again.

You'll want to run iPad-specific or universal apps when you can, to get the full use of the power of the iPad's far-larger screen. As the iPad user base grows, iPhone apps will likely be upgraded to support iPad as well, either in an iPad-specific or a dual-mode version.

CAUTION: **Stick with the App Store**

For most iPhone and iPad users, the only way to get apps is through Apple's App Store. A few users "jailbreak" their devices, allowing them to run non-App Store apps. However, if you do this, you violate your device's warranty, risk loss of access to the App Store, and open yourself up to potential problems, such as viruses and fraud.

Finding Out About Apps

Apple has made famous the line, "there's an app for that," to describe just how much apps can do for you. There are roughly 200,000 apps in Apple's App Store at this writing, so it's impossible for any user to research all of them, or even to carefully look into all the apps in most categories. Instead, people use several techniques to find apps, as follows:

- ▶ Reading ads, from Apple and others, that highlight apps

- ▶ Reading the press, including the specialized technology press

- ▶ Talking to friends, family members, and business colleagues

- ▶ Broad searches online (not in the App Store)

- ▶ Searching in the App Store through iTunes or on your iPad

I recommend that you use several, if not all, of these techniques congruently. By taking this approach, you'll get the "official" information and user reviews in the App Store, plus a wide range of other information and opinions from your broader search, all of which are needed to help you make good decisions on how to use your precious time, money (for apps that aren't free), and attention.

Apple has a web site for iPad apps at www.apple.com/ipad/apps-for-ipad, shown in Figure 11.2. Use this site to research and learn about some of the top apps for iPad. You can also use sites like Gizmodo, TechCrunch, Mashable, and many others. (It may prove to be helpful to search on an app name to find sites that have written about the app, and then search the sites you find in more depth to see what iPad apps they recommend.)

FIGURE 11.2   Apple's iPad Apps web site highlights top offerings.

One topic of particular interest is money. In many cases, you can get free apps that do at least the core things that a paid-for app does. You may also find a web site, perhaps one using HTML 5 to deliver video or other inter-active content, that you can visit for free from your iPad, and that does much or all of what an app does.

> TIP: **Use a Computer First**
>
> Do broad searches for information about apps on your personal computer; which gives you more screen space than the iPad and the ability to more easily move among multiple browser windows, then search in the App Store for the specific app.

Use your research to find free or lower-cost alternatives to paid apps. One site that highlights free apps is iPadLuv, at www.ipadluv.net.

Finding and Downloading Apps

There are two ways to get apps. One approach is to search in Apple's App Store using iTunes, and then download the app to iTunes. The next time you synchronize your iPad with your personal computer, the app is transferred to your iPad. Apps you purchase for your iPod Touch or iPhone will also be automatically synchronized to your iPad, and will work fine there.

However, many iPad users, including me, like to do as much directly on the iPad as reasonably possible. So, another approach is to find and download apps directly onto your iPad. This way, there's no waiting for your iPad to sync in order to use your app. The app will be backed up into iTunes on your personal computer the next time you sync.

In order to purchase apps or iTunes content, you need an iTunes account linked to a credit card or iTunes gift card. You will be asked to provide the relevant information if you try to download a paid app or paid content without having provided payment information. For instructions about using iTunes to sync any existing iPhone apps you already have onto your iPad, see Lesson 16, "Using iTunes to Sync Multimedia and More."

> NOTE: **Get an iTunes Account**
>
> You must have an iTunes store account to download applications. Go to Settings > Store to set up a new account if needed. See Lesson 16 for details.

Follow these steps to find apps in the App Store:

1. Tap the App Store app to start it.

2. Tap either the Featured, Top Charts, or Categories icon at the bottom of the screen to look for apps that interest you and fit your needs.

You can find various special designations like the App of the Week, Staff Favorites, and others. iPad-specific apps, which are the more desirable choice in most cases, are sometimes designated HD (for High Definition) or XL (for eXtra Large, referring to the iPad's larger screen), or have iPad in the name ("Twitterific for iPad" is an example). However, there is not always a specific iPad designation.

NOTE: **Redeem Your Codes**

If you have a redemption code for an app—for instance, one obtained from the developer's web site—use the Redeem button at the bottom of the Featured screen or the Top Charts screen; then enter the code.

---

3. Search using keywords to find apps of interest, or to find specific apps that you have learned about through research on your personal computer and elsewhere.

4. When you see an app you like on a page or in a list of search results, tap the brief description to see more. A full description appears on the Info screen, as shown in Figure 11.3.

5. To see customer ratings and reviews, scroll down. To see screenshots (where available), scroll down and then flick through screenshots. To see additional apps from the same developer (where available), scroll down and then look in the left-hand column.

FIGURE 11.3 App descriptions entice you to add ever more apps.

NOTE: **Use Ratings First**

The ratings and comments are quite helpful in understanding the strong and weak points of an app, including the specifics of how well it looks and works on iPad, as opposed to iPhone or other platforms it might run on.

---

6. To install the app on your iPad, press the button in the upper-left corner, which either says "Free" or has the app's price on it.

7. Enter your iTunes password.

The app starts downloading. You're taken to a page on your iPad's Home screen where the app icon appears, and you can watch the icon fill in as the app downloads.

NOTE: **Apps Downloads Recover**

If an app download is interrupted by a lost connection or a server problem, it resumes the next time you connect. Alternatively, you can open iTunes on your personal computer, and the app downloads to iTunes, and then is copied to your iPad the next time you sync.

CAUTION: **No Deposit, No Return**

At this writing, the App Store's return policy is: There are no returns, except if the App Store fails to deliver the app to you within a reasonable period of time. There is no trial period for apps you purchase. So, research apps carefully—including, if possible, trying the app out on the iPad of a friend who's already purchased it— before buying.

---

8. To use the app after it downloads, tap its icon.

Following Up After Installing an App

After you download an app and install it, you may need technical support, want to write a review, or want to share your opinion of the app with friends. The App Store supports all these needs:

▶ **Rating apps.** To rate the app, press the appropriate number of stars on the app's Info page and then enter any comments. See Figure 11.4 for examples of ratings for an app.

▶ **Reporting problems.** To report a problem with the app, press the Report a Problem link at the upper right of the screen. For app support, press the App Support button. (The difference between Report a Problem and App Support is not always clear, and varies from app to app.)

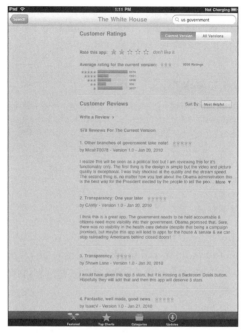

FIGURE 11.4 Rating apps is kind to others.

▶ **Updating applications.** The App Store icon displays a number on the icon to show any application updates that are available. To install the update(s), open the App Store, and press the Updates icon at the bottom of the screen. Then press the icon for each app that needs an update; the update will install.

▶ **Uninstalling.** To uninstall an app from iTunes, press and hold the app's icon until it wiggles onscreen; then tap the X that appears next to the icon. The app disappears from the screen, and its data is no longer accessible, but it isn't erased from iPad.

▶ **Clearing settings and data.** If you want, you can uninstall an app, and then "buy" it again in the App Store. (You shouldn't be charged again for the repeat "purchase" of a paid-for app.) Uninstalling and restoring has the effect of restoring the app to its default settings, minus any settings you've changed and data you've entered into the app. This is a commonly recommended way of solving problems with an app.

TIP: **App Store Keeps Track**

The App Store keeps track of which apps you install and/or buy. Any apps you download and install onto your iPad are copied into iTunes the next time you sync. So, there's no risk of losing track of an app once you download it, or of losing money you've spent on an app purchase.

Summary

In this lesson, you learned how to find out about apps, download and install them, and follow up by rating apps, reporting on problems, and updating them. In the next lesson, I show you how to get photos onto your iPad and view them.

Importing and Viewing Photos

*In this lesson, you learn how to import photos from your personal comput-
er or a digital camera or cellphone; how to get photos through screen
shots and downloading attachments; how to view photos onscreen, in
albums, as wallpaper, and in the Picture Frame feature; and how to share
photos.*

Photos on the iPad

The iPad might be the best device yet for storing, arranging, and sharing
photos. It is both easier to use and more powerful than the old-fashioned
photo album. The iPad displays digital photographs in a nice, large size—
much larger than viewing on a smartphone—beautifully backlit, and in full
color. At the same time, the iPad's thinness, light weight, and flexibility
make it easy to share photos with others.

Your iPad supports a wide range of photo formats, including the following:

▶ **JPEG.** JPEG is short for Joint Photographic Experts Group, a
   carefully crafted standard for compressing photo files by 90% or
   more with little visible loss of quality. If you are saving photos in
   JPEG format for use on the iPad from a graphics program such
   as Photoshop, consider using a resolution of about 150 dpi and
   roughly 80% compression.

CAUTION: **Don't Use JPEG Twice**

JPEG is great, but the current practice of compressing the same
photo through JPEG three or four times amplifies the worse effects

---

> of JPEG compression, so don't run them through JPEG compression
> more than once.

▶ **TIFF.** TIFF means Tagged Image File Format. TIFF is a lossless
format, so photographs are big (in file size) and beautiful. When
you get a JPEG file, and edit it, consider saving the result as
TIFF or PNG to avoid the degradation inherent in multiple JPEG
compression cycles.

▶ **GIF.** GIF, or Graphics Image Format, has small file sizes but is
limited to 256 colors and is very hard on any but black-and-white
images or the smallest photos. Avoid GIF for photos in most
cases. It's suitable for some simpler (in terms of color usage)
computer-generated images, though.

▶ **PNG.** PNG, originally defined as standing for "PNG's Not GIF,"
is much like GIF, but without the 256-color limitation. As a lossless format, without GIF's limitation to 256 colors, PNG is an
increasingly popular file format for images of all sorts.

The iPad's role with photos does highlight one of the criticisms of the
iPad: unlike a personal computer, it's used more for consuming media and
information than for creating it. The iPad doesn't have a camera in it.
Photos have to be taken on other devices and imported into the iPad, defi-
nitely leading to delayed gratification.

The iPad also suffers as a photo manager in comparison to a personal computer. The iPad resizes photos to fit the iPad screen. The iPad screen is big
enough that the resulting resized image is fine for most digital uses.
However, if you want to keep the original, higher-resolution file—and
especially if you ever plan to print the image at a typical photo size, such
as 4″ x 6″, or even larger—then don't use the iPad as the only repository
for your images.

In addition, there's a concern with storage space. Even a moderately compressed photo on the iPad takes up about 1MB of space. That's 1,000 photos per gigabyte, which sounds like a lot, but adds up pretty fast. This is
far less of a concern on a personal computer, with its hard disk that is
many times larger than the static RAM in an iPad.

If these concerns resonate for you, consider using your personal computer for your photo management tasks instead of the iPad. The iPad remains a great device for viewing and sharing photos. Use the information and steps in this lesson to help you get the most out of it.

CAUTION: **iPad Resizes Photos**

When iPad imports photos, it resizes them as necessary to fit its screen. This is fine for viewing photos on iPad. However, if keeping the original, highest-resolution version of the images is important to you, don't use iPad as your storage device.

Synchronizing Photos with Other Devices

The original iPod music player, used with iTunes software, depended on a personal computer as the organizing hub for music files. As the iPod line added movies, phone capabilities (the iPhone), and now the enhanced capabilities of the iPad, this personal computer-centric organizing principle has remained.

If you use a personal computer as a kind of media control panel, your life with your iPad is easy. Just continue bringing photos to your personal computer, from one or more devices, then sync your iPad to your personal computer using iTunes. (Syncing using iTunes is described in Lesson 16, "Using iTunes to Sync Multimedia and More.")

You can also sync digital photos directly from a camera, cellphone, or SD memory card. To do this, you need the iPad Camera Connection Kit, described in Lesson 1, "Introducing iPad."

NOTE: **USB Just for Cameras**

The USB Camera Connector only supports cameras, not other USB devices.

Follow these steps to sync digital photos using the iPad Camera Connection Kit:

1. Insert the SD Card Reader or USB Camera Connector into the iPad dock connector port.

2. For an SD memory card, insert it into the slot on the SD Card Reader. For a camera, iPhone, or other cellphone that takes pictures, use that device's USB cable to connect to the USB Camera Connector. Make sure the device is turned on and, if applicable, in transfer mode.

   For the SD memory card, insert the card gently, as it will only fit in one orientation. (For other devices, see the device's documentation for details.)

   Your iPad automatically opens the Photos application and displays the photos that it can import from the device or SD card you've connected.

3. To import all of the photos, tap Import All. To import specific photos, tap the photo's thumbnail image to place checkmarks next to the ones you want; then tap Import.

   The photos are imported to your iPad, which may take a few seconds (see Figure 12.1).

4. Choose whether to keep or delete the photos on the device or SD card you've connected.

5. Disconnect the SD Card Reader or USB Camera Connector.

6. View the photos in the Last Import album in the Photos app.

7. Transfer the photos to your personal computer by connecting the iPad to the personal computer using USB and importing the images with a photo program, such as Adobe Photoshop Elements or Apple's iPhoto.

TIP: **Get Rid of Extra Photos**

Consider developing a routine for transferring photos to your iPad, and possibly other devices, and then deleting them from the original device at some point in the process, so the original device doesn't fill up with photo files.

FIGURE 12.1   Photos come to life on iPad.

Viewing Photos on the iPad

Viewing photos on iPad is enjoyable. I've already seen a professional photographer buy several simply for use as a highly capable and flexible photo frame.

There are several ways you can view photos on iPad:

- ▶ One at a time, within the Photos option of the Photos app.

- ▶ One at a time, within an Album in the Albums option of the Photos app.

- ▶ One at a time, within a group of photos taken in a specific place, in the Places option of the Photos app. (Shows all geo-tagged photos taken in a specific place.)

- ▶ One at a time, within the Events or Faces option of the Photos app. (These two categories must be configured in either the iPhoto or Aperture application on a Macintosh personal computer, and then added to the iPad by syncing it to the Mac. These options are not available on Windows PCs.)

- ▶ As a slideshow within any option of the Photos app.

- ▶ As screen wallpaper on the Home screen, the Lock screen, or both.

- ▶ Using the Picture Frame option of the Lock screen to go through all your photos, or all the photos in a given Album or other category.

Using an appropriate connector, such as those described in Lesson 1, you can display photos on a TV or projector for viewing by many people.

Follow the steps in this section to manage the display of photos on your iPad.

> CAUTION: **Managing iPad Photos**
>
> You cannot delete photos on iPad, nor can you rearrange them into different folders. This is annoying when you have one or two photos that you really don't want to show a lot of people, embedded

among photos that you do want to share. To manage the photos on iPad, make changes in your photo files and folders on your personal computer and then re-sync using iTunes, as described in Lesson 16.

Getting Photos as Screenshots and Attachments

Although most photos come to your computer by transferring them from your personal computer and other devices, there are two ways to get photos onto your iPad that don't necessarily apply to other devices: as email attachments, and as iPad screenshots.

When you get an email, the photo shows up as an attachment icon in the body of the email. To download it, tap the icon. The photo downloads.

To save or copy the image, tap it. Options appear to enable you to save the image or copy it, as shown in Figure 12.2. (You can do the same with images on websites; be careful, though, not to violate copyright in your use of images obtained in this way.)

You can also create images by taking a screenshot of whatever is on the iPad screen, such as a web site you are viewing. Just hold down the Home button, and then press the Sleep/Wake button. The current screen contents are captured.

For email attachments and screenshots, images are saved into the Saved Photos folder.

TIP: **Create Your Own Zoomed Photo**
Some iPad features enable you to pan and zoom before saving a photo. You can also use panning and zooming to edit your photos on iPad. Just bring up a photo for viewing, as described in the next section. Then pan (by dragging) and zoom (by pinching) to get the appearance you want. Take a screenshot of the result and use it as

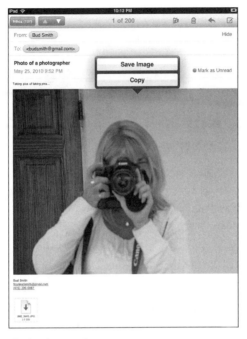

FIGURE 12.2   Saving images is easy.

a photo of its own. The resolution will be somewhat lower, depending on how much you've zoomed, but the result may still look very good indeed.

Viewing Photos

You can view photos in several different ways in the Photos app. When you open the Photos app, you have the choice of viewing your photos as Photos, Albums, or Places. (They are also viewed as Events or Faces, if you use iPhoto or Aperture on a Mac to create these categories.) The following outlines how each category works:

▶ If you choose Photos, you simply see a large array of photos, as shown previously in Figure 12.1.

▶ If you choose Albums, you see photos grouped by date. You can spread an Album to view the photos in it, as shown in Figure 12.3.

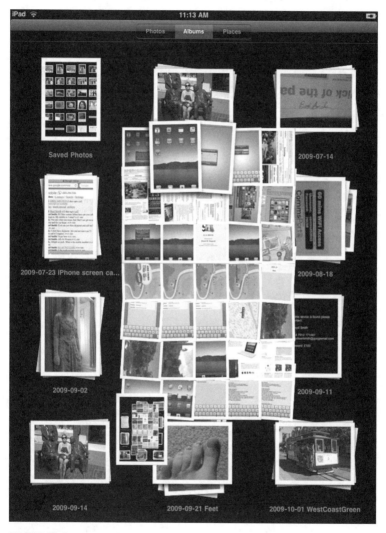

FIGURE 12.3   A set of folders, with the middle folder spread to show its contents.

▶ If you choose Places, you see a map with pins showing where your geo-referenced photos were taken, as shown in Figure 12.4. (Some cameras, including some smartphone cameras, include geo-referencing information in photos automatically.) Touch a pin to see the initial photo for that location; spread the group of photos with your fingers to preview the group.

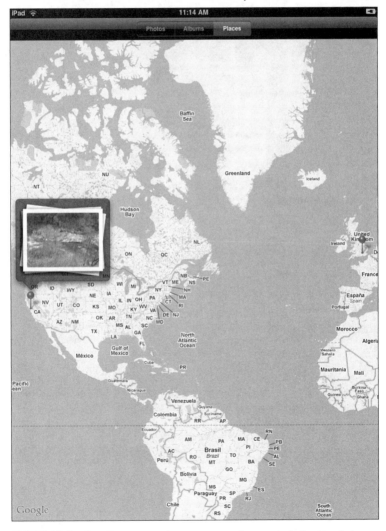

FIGURE 12.4 The Photos app gives you geo-referenced photo groupings.

Viewing and Sharing Individual Photos

When you view an individual photo from any source, it fits the screen in its current orientation. Move the screen to a horizontal or vertical orientation as needed to best fit the photo.

The photo is shown without controls for maximum impact—when you tap the screen, controls are shown. Here are the controls available:

▶ **Zoom and pan.** You can pinch your fingers together on the screen to zoom in, unpinch to zoom back out, and then drag to pan within the picture. You can actually make the photo quite different just by zooming and panning around within it. For high-resolution photos, the quality is maintained even when you zoom in close. You can then take a screenshot, as described later in this section, to create a new photo from the old one. This self-created shot may be useful for emailing, for instance, since you don't otherwise have the option to edit a photo before sending it.

▶ **Choose from photos in a folder.** To move to another photo in the same folder, tap the photo; controls appear that enable you to move to other photos, as shown in Figure 12.4. Then tap the photo you want in the strip at the bottom. (This feature is not very useful in folders with dozens of photos or more, as is likely to be the case for the Photos tab within the Photos app, for instance. However, you can get more selective power by pressing and holding on the strip, and then dragging the highlight slowly from one photo to the next.)

▶ **Create a slideshow.** To view a folder's photos in a slideshow, tap the Slideshow button. Slideshow options appear, as shown in Figure 12.5. Use the options to play music or not, and to choose the music to play. Also choose transition effects, such as Cube, Dissolve, Ripple, Wipe, or Origami; try them all to see which ones you like. To change other settings—the length of time each slide plays, whether the slideshow repeats, and whether to shuffle photos randomly in the slideshow—go to Settings > Photos. (The defaults are 3 seconds per slide, no repeating, and the shuffle function turned off.)

FIGURE 12.5 You can return to the containing folder, start a slideshow, email a photo, and use other options, or move among photos in the current folder.

TIP: **Get the Most Out of Slideshows**

Creating slideshows can take considerable time and effort to get the folder contents right before setting up the slideshow. However, the effect of slideshows on your photos is wonderful, and even a simple slideshow with seemingly ordinary photos can be very powerful. You can also view your slideshows on various external displays with an appropriate connector for your iPad.

Tap the Share icon to open up additional options, as shown in Figure 12.6. The options available are as follows:

▶ **Email Photo.** An email message with the photo in it opens. You can address the email, enter a subject line, and add text.

▶ **Assign to Contact.** iPad gives you a great opportunity to assign a photo to a contact. Tap Assign to Contact, then choose the contact to save the photo with. The Photo app then lets you pan and zoom the photo to select just the part that you want to assign to your contact. Click Use when you're done, and the cropped section of the photo will be used for your contact. If you have your contacts synced to other platforms, as described in Lesson 7, "Synching, Sending, and Receiving Email," the photo will appear on those platforms as well.

▶ **Use as Wallpaper.** You can use a photo as wallpaper for your lock screen, your home screen, or both. Pan and zoom to get the look of the photo the way you want it; then click the appropriate Set button.

▶ **Copy Photo.** You can copy a photo for use in various applications.

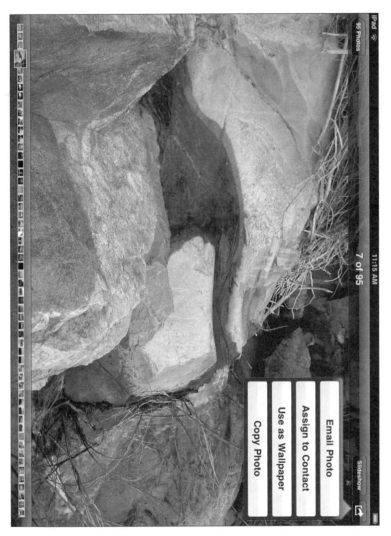

FIGURE 12.6   You have the option to email a photo, assign it to a contact, use it as wallpaper for the home or lock screens, or copy a photo.

Using Picture Frame

Picture Frame is a novel iPad application that's similar to the screensaver functionality available on many personal computers. However, the look and feel of the iPad and its screen gives the photos in Picture Frame great impact.

Follow these steps to set up Picture Frame:

1. Go to Settings, Picture Frame. Picture Frame has different settings than the Photos app has.

2. Choose a transition effect—Dissolve or Origami.

3. Choose whether to zoom in on faces.

    If you turn on this option, iPad finds and zooms in on faces while displaying slides in the Picture Frame.

4. Choose All Photos, or choose specific albums. Press Albums to see available albums, as shown in Figure 12.7. Choose the albums you want displayed. Clear the checkmarks next to the albums you don't want displayed.

5. To start or stop Picture Frame, press the Sleep/Wake button to lock your iPad. From the Lock screen, tap the Picture Frame button to bring the Picture Frame onscreen.

    Picture Frame begins displaying photos.

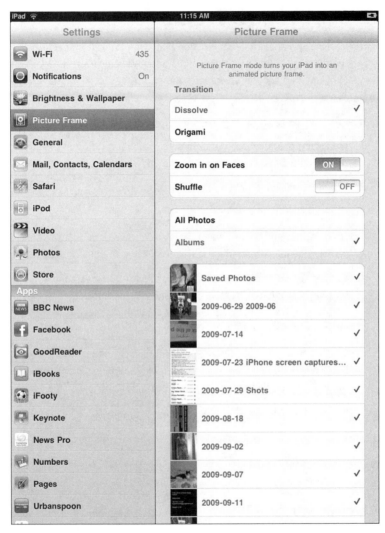

FIGURE 12.7   Picture Frame has settings of its own.

Summary

In this lesson, you learned how to use photos on the iPad, including importing them, taking screenshots, sharing them, and viewing them in albums and in the Picture Frame. In the next lesson, I show you how to play videos on your iPad.

LESSON 13

Playing Videos and YouTube

In this lesson, you learn about the many kinds of video you can play on your iPad, how to play many kinds of stored videos, and how to find and play YouTube videos.

About Videos and YouTube

The progress of video seems to be going to two extremes: In many homes, large, flat-screen TVs are used to show hundreds of channels, with the selection fed by ever more expensive cable and satellite television services. On the other end of the spectrum is the iPad, a small, highly portable device, far less expensive to operate and with much less impact on the environment.

Many people are making greater and greater use of a la carte video. The iPad is arguably the best device, and iTunes and YouTube among the best delivery vehicles, for this new way of accessing video.

With iPad, you can view many kinds of video, as follows:

- ▶ Movies
- ▶ Music videos
- ▶ Video podcasts
- ▶ TV shows
- ▶ Special videos created for use on digital devices

These videos are accessed several different ways as well:

- ▶ The iTunes store, which is very efficient and has a lot of great content, especially movies and TV shows you can buy or rent.

- ▶ Web sites, such as TV channel sites, which offer many shows for free, others for a fee.

- ▶ Movie and video subscription services such as Netflix that increasingly offer streaming services.

- ▶ YouTube, which includes many videos made and distributed for use on digital devices such as iPad.

- ▶ Innumerable sites with access to large or small amounts of video—some general, some specialized. Many use the emerging HTML 5 standard, and are referred to as HTML 5 video-enabled web sites.

This lesson explains how to find videos, how to play videos stored on your iPad, and how to play videos from the YouTube site.

Playing Videos

One thing to be aware of when using videos on iPad is the considerable amount of time it takes to download video. It's hardly "instant gratification." Even with a broadband connection, it can easily take about half the time to download a video that it takes to watch it. So, for a two-hour movie, plan on the download taking approximately an hour. (This is the same whether you download the video to your iPad first, or to your personal computer first, then make the much quicker transfer from your personal computer to your iPad.)

You need to plan your video purchases or rentals in advance, so that the downloading is completed before you're ready to watch.

> TIP: **Save Your Rental Time**
> When downloading a rental, be aware that the rental time doesn't start until you actually start playing the movie. So, don't start

playing it back just to check that it works. Instead, wait until you're
ready to watch at least a good part of the video.

Another constraint to consider is the limited amount of storage space on
the iPad—roughly a tenth to a fourth of what you'll find on a typical personal computer. The best strategy for managing this issue is to store videos
on your personal computer and then sync them to your iPad selectively.
See Lesson 16, "Using iTunes to Sync Multimedia and More," for information on how to get and sync videos to your iPad. Once you have videos
on your iPad, playing them back is easy:

1. Tap Videos to start the app.

2. Choose a category that has videos in it, such as Movies or TV
   Shows. The available videos display. Related videos may be
   grouped together, and longer videos may be grouped into chapters.
   For instance, if you have several episodes of a TV show, an icon
   showing the TV show, not the individual episodes, may display.

3. If necessary, tap the icon for a group of videos, such as episodes
   in a TV series.

   The individual episodes display. An example is seen in
   Figure 13.1.

4. To play the video, tap its icon.

5. To control the video, tap the screen. The controls for the video
   display, as shown in Figure 13.2. To hide the controls, tap the
   screen again, or wait a few seconds and they will disappear on
   their own.

6. You can tap Pause to stop the video and then tap Play to resume
   playing it. Press and hold the Rewind or Fast Forward icons to
   move to the beginning or end of the video or chapter; or drag the
   volume slider at the bottom of the screen to change the playback
   volume.

7. To get to a specific spot in the video, drag the slider along the top
   to the spot you want. This slider is called the "scrubber bar," and

FIGURE 13.1   You can store an entire series of a favorite show on the iPad.

you can slow down its speed of movement—the "scrub rate"—by dragging your finger from the scrubber bar down the screen. When you reach the bottom of the screen, the scrub rate slows to nearly a frame-by-frame rate.

8. You can also pause a video without using its controls in order to do something else on your iPad, such as read an email. While a video is playing, tap Home and open a different app. The video pauses. When you return to it, it will resume where you left off.

9. When you're finished watching the video, tap Done. The screen returns to the list of videos that contains the video you were watching.

10. To delete a video, press and hold on its icon until the X button appears for deleting it. Tap the X button.

The video is deleted from iPad, but will remain available for re-download or transfer from your personal computer via iTunes. See Lesson 16 for details.

FIGURE 13.2   The iPad displays control functions onscreen.

NOTE: **Watch on a Bigger Screen**

To watch videos or YouTube from your iPad on a computer moni-tor, TV, or projector, use an Apple iPad Dock Connector, Apple Component AV Cable, or Apple Composite AV Cable, as described in Lesson 1.

Finding and Playing YouTube Videos

YouTube is an amazing resource for videos. It contains a great deal of recent cultural history—including broadcast videos (or clips from them), in addition to videos recorded primarily for use with YouTube or other online sites.

You can only use YouTube if you have an active Internet connection. So, if you plan to watch videos while away from reliable Internet access, they must first be downloaded.

Some features of YouTube will work better for you if you have a YouTube account. To sign up for an account, visit the YouTube site at www. youtube.com. (On the iPad, this needs to be done in a web browser. The YouTube site cannot be accessed through the YouTube app.)

There are several ways to get to YouTube videos on your iPad:

▶ **Web site embedding.** Many videos on different web sites are hosted on YouTube, but you see them embedded in the web site you're visiting.

▶ **Web site links.** Many web sites link to videos for playback on the YouTube site, either in conjunction with embedding them on the site with the link, or only via the link.

▶ **The YouTube site.** Visit the YouTube site in your web browser and play back videos there. The YouTube app offers easier access to YouTube features, particularly if you have a YouTube account.

▶ **The YouTube app.** YouTube is a built-in app on every iPad, and is very easy to use.

▶ **Search.** Search is really powerful on YouTube. If you don't believe me, just try a search for "skateboard dog," and be prepared to spend an hour or so laughing at videos of dogs on skateboards.

▶ **Categories.** The YouTube app offers easy access to several categories of videos: Featured videos, Top Rated, Most Viewed, Favorites that you've marked, and a History of videos you've viewed. You are also offered access to features that require you to have an account: Your subscriptions and videos you've created and uploaded to YouTube (My Videos).

▶ **Related videos.** Once you find and play back a video, YouTube offers easy access to related videos. This is probably the leading feature of YouTube that entices people to spend hours watching YouTube videos when they should be doing something—almost anything—else.

CAUTION: **Connect to the Internet for YouTube**

You can only use YouTube when you have an Internet connection, and a slow or intermittent Internet connection may cause problems with video playback.

Playing a YouTube video is similar to playing a stored video, as described in the previous section, but with a few differences. Here's a brief overview:

▶ **Short videos.** YouTube videos are more limited in length. YouTube generally has a 10-minute limit, and most videos are much shorter than that.

▶ **Internet access matters.** Spotty Internet access will cause problems with the video playback, and no Internet access means no YouTube access, either via the YouTube app or the YouTube web site.

▶ **Landscape rules.** Watch YouTube videos with your iPad in landscape mode for best effect.

▶ **FullScreen is an option.** The usual YouTube display shows a video, comments about it, and related videos (see Figure 13.3). To see just the video, tap the FullScreen button. The video fills the screen.

▶ **View/Hide controls.** During video playback, the controls disappear, in order for you to see the video fully. Tap the screen to see controls, and tap it again to hide them.

▶ **Favoritize frequently.** Add a video to your Favorites by tapping the Favorites button.

▶ **Email a link.** Use the Email control to email a video link to a friend. Add the email address, the subject, and/or desired comments, and send.

▶ See **Related** videos, **More From** the video's maker, and **Comments**. Tap the appropriate button to access these additional features.

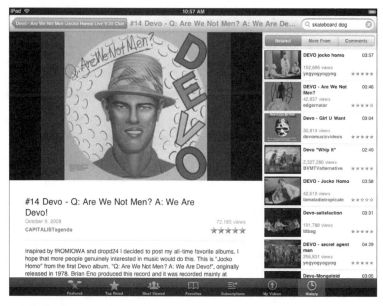

FIGURE 13.3   YouTube offers lots of related content and options.

▶ **Rate,** or leave a Comment. Tap Rate to rate a video and/or add a comment. (You have to be logged into an account to rate or comment on videos.)

▶ **Subscribe.** If you're logged into your account, you can subscribe to videos from the current video's maker.

Summary

In this lesson, you learned about the many kinds of video you can play on your iPad, how to play them, and how to find and play YouTube videos. In the next lesson, I show you how to use the iPod app to manage music.

LESSON 14

Using iPad for Music and More

In this lesson, you learn about how music works on iPad and how to play music, podcasts, and audiobooks, as well as how to create regular and Genius playlists.

Playing Music and Other Audio Files

The iPad's music app is called iPod, and the app works just like an iPod device. The iPod—whether it's the physical device or the app—is not really complete in and of itself. It's just one of a few crucial elements in a system that allows music and other audio content to be created, distributed—sometimes for free, sometimes for a price—played back, and managed.

To play audio files from the iPad app, you can use four different means:

▶ **iPad's built-in speakers.** The iPad has built-in speakers that, considering their small size and thinness, produce surprisingly good sound.

▶ **External speakers.** External speakers produce better results through their larger size and, for two-piece stereo speakers, greater separation. The iPad Dock (described in Lesson 1, "Introducing iPad") has an audio line-out port that enables you to connect to external speakers.

▶ **Wired headphones.** Headphones give even better results by bringing the sound closer to your ears and providing stereo separation, especially as the best (and most expensive) ones also cut out ambient noise. Even simple, inexpensive wired headphones give surprisingly good sound. You can even plug just the audio jack of audio/microphone combo headphones into the iPad's audio out jack and get sound. However, somewhat more expensive wired headphones from Apple and others give noticeably better sound.

▶ **Wireless Bluetooth headphones.** Wireless Bluetooth headphones can be paired to the iPad, as described in Lesson 4, "Getting Connected to Wi-Fi, 3G, and Bluetooth." Even the less-expensive ones give you a great deal of freedom and flexibility, and more advanced Bluetooth headphones with features like noise cancellation provide excellent sound.

Finding a Song by Category

To play a song, you first need to get to its icon in iPad, as follows:

1. Tap the iPod icon to start the app.

2. Choose a category that has audio in it, such as Music, Podcasts, or Audiobooks. You can also use the buttons at the bottom to look in categories—Songs, Artists, Albums, Genres, and Composers.

3. Tap the icon for an album, if needed, to see the songs that belong to it.

4. Tap the icon for a song. The song plays, displaying the album cover art, as shown in Figure 14.1.

TIP: **Keeping Music Alive**
You can press the Home button to find and use another app while the song plays.

FIGURE 14.1   Finding and playing songs on the iPad is easy.

Finding a Song by Searching

You can also find a song by searching for it:

1. Tap the Search box. Tap X to clear any previous entries. The on-screen keyboard opens to allow you to enter search text.

Enter something to search on. It can be a word from the song title or album, or the name of the artist or composer. Spelling matters, but capitalization doesn't. Search does not work inside names—for instance, "ach" won't find Bach, although "bac" will. If no valid results are found, the words "No Results" will display—even before you tap Search.

2. Tap the Search button on the keyboard to clear the keyboard and display final results.

The search might find valid results in any of the four categories: Songs, Artists, Albums, Genres, or Composers. (For instance, a search for "Mothers" might find both the artists, the Mothers of

Invention, and the composer Mark Mothersbaugh of Devo.) The categories in which valid results are found among your music selection are shown in normal text, and the categories in which no valid results are found are shown in grayed-out text.

You see results immediately if the category you had selected before the search began has valid search results; you see the words "No Results" if none of the categories has a valid result.

3. Tap category names that aren't grayed-out to view results.

Results are displayed, as shown in Figure 14.2.

FIGURE 14.2   Search helps you find your songs.

TIP: **Search with Short Strings**

Begin your search by entering just three or four letters of a search string. Unless you have an astoundingly large music collection, a short string is often enough to bring up your desired result.

Playing Back Songs

While a song is playing back, the Now Playing screen appears, as shown in Figure 14.3. This control gives you several options, as follows:

▶ **Volume.** Use the slider in the upper-left corner of the iPad screen or the physical volume control on your iPad to change the volume. You may also have a volume control on your headphones, which may or may not override the volume controls for your iPad.

▶ **Pause/Play.** When a song is playing, the Pause control appears; when you tap Pause, the Play control replaces it.

▶ **Advance/Rewind.** On either side of the Pause/Play controls, the Rewind and Advance controls are available. Tap Rewind to start at the song's beginning, and then repeatedly to move back

FIGURE 14.3   You can get iPod controls when using another app by double-pressing Home.

through previous songs. Tap Advance to move to the beginning of
the next song and then again to move through subsequent songs.

▶ **Move ahead/back.** During playback, a round ball indicates the
current location of playback in the song. Drag the ball backward
or forward to move to a different spot in the song.

▶ **Playback list.** Tap the album art icon in the main list to see a
playlist. Tap beside the playlist to return to seeing the album art
icon in the main list.

▶ **Album art.** Tap the album art icon under Now Playing to see it
full-size. Pinch the full-size album art to return to the usual playback screen.

▶ **Controlling your music.** When you're listening to music while
using another app, double-press the Home button to display
playback controls without leaving the current app, as shown in
Figure 14.3. (If you double-press the Home button while already
in the iPod app, or while not listening to music, the Search screen
for the iPod appears instead.)

Playing Back Podcasts and Audiobooks

While a podcast or audiobook is playing back, additional controls appear,
as shown in Figure 14.4:

▶ **Repeat.** Tap to repeat the content indefinitely.

▶ **Scrubbing.** As with videos (see Lesson 13, "Playing Videos and
YouTube"), you can change the rate of forwarding or rewinding,
an action referred to as "scrubbing." This is done by dragging
your finger down the screen as you move it ahead of or behind
the current play point in the content.

▶ **Playback speed.** Tap the 1x button to change the playback speed
among 1x, 2x, and 1/2x. Normally, fast playback makes speech
high-pitched and unpleasant, but the iPod app automatically
adjusts the pitch to make it easy to listen to, even at high speeds.

▶ **Skip.** You can skip back in the content by a predefined amount
by tapping the skip button.

FIGURE 14.4   Podcasts and audiobooks have additional controls.

Using Playlists

Playlists are collections you make of your own songs. You can use them to create a mood, to power a party, or for any other purpose you can think of. Playlists are one of the secrets of the success of the iPod device and the iPod capability on the iPhone and iPad.

A Genius playlist is a special feature that creates playlists by searching for songs that go well together. The Genius feature works best if you have a large and eclectic playlist—so large that you don't even get around to playing some of your songs. A Genius playlist will often dig up these undiscovered gems, mixing them with other songs in interesting ways.

Creating Playlists

Although you may put a lot of thought into creating a playlist, the actual steps you need to follow to create the list are easy, as follows:

1. In the iPod app, tap + at the bottom of the screen.

2. Enter a name for the playlist, and then tap Save. iPod lists all your songs.

3. Tap the + button to add a song to your playlist. Alternatively, you can look in Artists, Albums, Genres, or Composers to find songs to add. Tap Sources to browse among different kinds of sources, as shown in Figure 14.5.

FIGURE 14.5   Playlists can draw on all your sources.

4. Tap Done when finished. The next time you sync with your personal computer, your playlist will be saved in iTunes as well.

5. To edit the playlist, tap Edit, and then drag the box next to each selection to move it up or down in the list. Tap – next to the selection to remove it, tap Add Songs and tap the + button next to songs to add them, or tap – next to the playlist name to remove the entire playlist. See Figure 14.6 for an example of a playlist being edited.

FIGURE 14.6   Playlists are easy to edit.

Creating Genius Playlists

To use the Genius function, you need to first turn on the Genius function in iTunes. In iTunes, look for the Genius icon in the left-hand tray. Click the icon to turn on the feature; for details, see Lesson 16.

Once the Genius feature is enabled, creating a Genius playlist is easy. Just tap the Genius button—the atomic-looking button shown in Figure 14.5— and then tap New. Choose a song in the list. Genius creates a playlist of similar songs from your collection. Tap Save; the playlist is created, with the name of the song that you were viewing when you created it.

You can refresh your Genius playlist to incorporate different songs, or new songs that you've added to your collection. Simply tap Refresh in the Genius playlist. You can also delete Genius playlists.

The process sounds kind of random, but people with large song collections often report surprising success with Genius.

Genius also searches your iPad library and creates Genius Mixes, each of which taps into a different type of music. To play a Genius Mix, just tap its name.

Summary

In this lesson, you learned how to play music, podcasts, and audiobooks on your iPad, as well as how to create regular and Genius playlists. In the next lesson, I show you how to use iBooks and the iBookstore.

Using iBooks and the iBookstore

In this lesson, you learn about reading iBooks on your iPad, and using the iBookstore and other sources to get free and paid-for books for your iPad.

Introducing iBooks

The iBooks app is the iPad's book-reading software. An iBook is a book specially formatted for use in the iBooks app on the iPad. Unlike a printed book, an iBook can contain multimedia content such as video clips.

There's a lot of excitement about iBooks, for many different reasons. One important reason is the size, shape, and weight of the iPad. It's quite similar to the page size of many books. Another reason is the large, bright, colorful screen of the iPad, all adorning a device meant to be held in one's hands, like a book. You, as the reader, can get as close to the content as you want, without strain. You get to experience full-color illustrations, animations, and video, unlike many of the e-reading devices available today.

Adversely, the weight of the iPad, at one and a half pounds, is about 50% heavier than a typical, 300-page softcover book.

Like other electronic devices used for reading, the iPad offers great search capabilities—a feature readers of printed books have long wished for. However, unlike most other e-reading devices, with iPad, you also have access to the full Internet experience on the same device as your e-books. An e-book can link to the Internet, incorporate Internet content, be updated over the Internet, and much more.

You can buy books to use with the iBooks app directly from your iPad or from iTunes running on your personal computer. Synchronizing the two copies the book from your iPad to the iTunes software running on your PC, or vice versa. See Lesson 16, "Using iTunes to Sync Multimedia and More," for details.

As described more fully in the "Finding and Buying Books" section later in this lesson, you can also get books in ePub format, a widely used industry standard, to use in iBooks. Many book reader programs and browser add-ons for personal computers support ePub, as do devices such as Sony Reader, the Barnes & Noble nook e-book reader, and phones and devices using Google's Android operating system. You can drag and drop ePub books into iTunes on your computer, and you can then sync them to your iPad, as described in Lesson 16.

Reading Books

You can read a sample iBook before buying or downloading one of your choosing. The iBooks app comes with one or more books you can use to get started.

Follow these steps to read an iBook:

1. Press iBooks to start the app.

2. Find the book you want to read; then tap to open it.

   Once open, you see either the cover, the Table of Contents, the first page of content, or a page to which the book was previously open.

3. To get a feel for the look of the book as it would appear if it were a physical book in your hands, hold the iPad horizontally. To fill the screen with a single page, hold the iPad vertically.

   The look changes as you move from horizontal to vertical. Doing this is important for illustrated books and other books with carefully laid-out page spreads, such as the Winnie the Pooh book that comes with iPad.

4. To scroll through the book's pages one at a time, swipe to the left or right.

5. To bookmark a word, look it up in the Dictionary, or use it for searching, press and hold the word. (You don't bookmark a page or a paragraph in iBooks, you bookmark a specific word.)

The word is highlighted, and a menu of options appears: Dictionary, Bookmark, and Search, as shown in Figure 15.1. The Dictionary option brings up a (non-context-specific) definition of the word; for instance, looking up the name "Christopher" in Winnie the Pooh brings up a reference to former U.S. Secretary of State Warren Christopher, but nothing about Christopher Robin. Searching brings up a list of all references to that word in the currently open book, as described in steps 15 and 16.

FIGURE 15.1 Start by selecting to look up a word in the Dictionary, Bookmark it, or Search for it.

6. Choose the Bookmark option to bookmark the word. The word then appears in yellow highlighter color, and a bookmark to the word is added to the Bookmarks list.

7. To change the bookmark color of a bookmarked word, or to change the bookmarking color for that word and subsequent bookmarks, press and hold on the word. Choose Unbookmark to remove the word from the bookmarks list. Choose the new bookmarking color from the list that appears to change the color highlighting of that word.

8. To prevent the page from flipping between horizontal and vertical mode, get the screen display the way you like it and turn on the Screen Rotation Lock on the side of your iPad.

The screen won't rotate again until you turn off the Screen Rotation Lock.

9. To see controls, if they're not already visible, tap the screen.

Controls appear across the top of the screen, as shown in Figure 15.2. You can always make controls disappear and re-appear by tapping the screen.

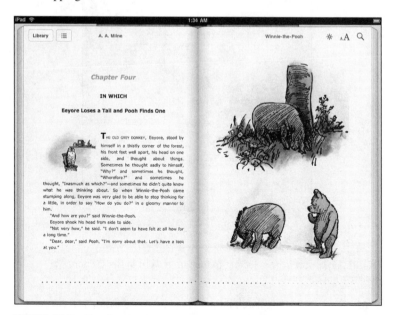

FIGURE 15.2   Reading books, like playing songs, is easy and fun.

10. To return to the Library, tap the Library button in the upper-left corner. This closes the book and re-opens the Library.

11. To bring up the Table of Contents, tap the Table of Contents button located next to the Library button.

The Table of Contents appears, as shown in Figure 15.3. A Resume button also appears in the upper-right corner. You can press the Resume button to return to your previous page. The Resume button disappears when you return to the content.

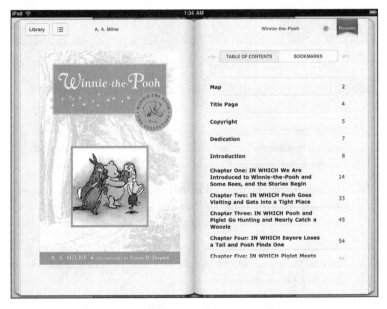

FIGURE 15.3   The Table of Contents and Bookmarks features give you quick access to the book's content.

12. To move directly into the book from the Table of Contents, tap any entry.

13. To switch to the Bookmarks list, tap the Table of Contents button at the top of the page to return to the page shown in Figure 15.2. Tap the Bookmarks button, and then choose a bookmark.

Alternatively, press Resume to return to your former place in the book.

To see all the entries in a long Table of Contents or Bookmarks list, drag to scroll up and down.

14. To change the brightness level, tap the Brightness button in the upper-right corner.

TIP: **iBooks-specific Brightness**

The iBooks Brightness feature is available in iBooks only. When you leave the iBooks app, your iBooks brightness setting will be ignored.

A slider appears that enables you to change the brightness level.

15. To change the font and font size, tap the Font button located in the upper-right corner.

You're presented with controls to make the font size bigger and smaller, as shown in Figure 15.4. As you make changes, the text reflows to suit your preferences.

16. To search for a specific word in the book, tap the Search icon. Enter a search term in the window that appears, and then tap the Search button in the onscreen keyboard.

A list of search results for the iBook appears. To search on a term you find in the text instead, press and hold it; then choose Search from the options that appear.

17. To continue your search on the Web (Internet connection required), change the search terms if needed, and then press the Search Google button or the Search Wikipedia button at the bottom of the search box.

The Safari web browser opens and search results appear. Google searches the entire Web, whereas Wikipedia only searches the Wikipedia online dictionary.

18. To scroll through the book's pages quickly, use the slider at the bottom of the screen.

FIGURE 15.4 You can easily change fonts and sizes.

TIP: **Saving Your Page in iBooks**

You can keep your place in a book and still close it to return to the Library, or press the Home button to return to the Home screen. Your book opens to the page you were last on when you return to it. To start the book fresh when you return, use the slider to go back to the front cover or Table of Contents before you exit the book.

Using the Bookshelf

You can use the Bookshelf to browse your books, or to delete a book. Follow these steps to work with the Bookshelf:

1. Tap the iBooks app icon to start it and, if the app opens to a book rather than the Bookshelf, tap the Library button to return to the Bookshelf.

2. Tap the list button to sort your books, and then select a sorting criterion from among the options on the bottom of the screen –

Titles, Authors, and Categories (such as fiction). The books are
sorted and displayed in a list, as shown in Figure 15.5. Push the
Bookshelf button to return to the Bookshelf.

FIGURE 15.5 Books in your Library can be displayed in a list.

3. Tap the Bookshelf view button to return to viewing your books in
   the Bookshelf.

4. To delete a book from the Bookshelf, tap Edit, or press and hold
   on any book's cover until the books start to shake. Tap the X on
   the cover of each book you want to delete, and it disappears.
   Then tap Edit again or press Home. The books stop shaking, and
   the delete (X button) controls disappear from the book icons.

If in the future, you change your mind about a book you've previously
deleted and you've synced your iPad to your personal computer, you can

re-download the book to iPad from iTunes on your personal computer. If the book you deleted was obtained via iBookstore, you can download it again from the Purchases tab in the Bookstore, as described later in this lesson.

NOTE: **Deleting Books From the Bookshelf**

When you delete a book from your Bookshelf, it will always be available for re-download to your iPad, either by syncing with iTunes on your personal computer or from the Purchases tab in the iBookstore. This enables you to delete any books you want from your Bookshelf without fear of thereby permanently losing them.

Finding and Buying Books

Books for iPad can be accessed in three ways:

▶ From the iPad, you can get books from iBookstore. You can't get books from web sites, as email attachments, or by any other means.

▶ From your personal computer, one way to get books is to buy the book through iTunes. It's then transferred to your iPad the next time you sync; see Lesson 16 for details.

▶ Also from your personal computer, you can get books in ePub format by downloading them from web sites, as email attachments, etc. Then drag and drop the ePub-formatted file into iTunes. The book is then transferred to your iPad the next time you sync; see Lesson 16 for details.

The sections that follow describe all of these ways to get books.

TIP: **Getting Free Books**

There are many free books available directly from the iBookstore, including the huge catalog of more than 30,000 free, out-of-copyright books from Project Gutenberg (www.gutenberg.org), which showcases many classics. The most-downloaded free books are listed via the Top Charts button of iBookstore. There are, in addition, many free books available in the ePub format, but many of these books are not available directly from the iBookstore. You have to download such books on your personal computer and then use iTunes to sync them to your iPad, as described in the next lesson.

Finding Books in iBookstore

To find a book in iBookstore, tap the Store button from the Bookshelf. iBookstore will open, as shown in Figure 15.6.

FIGURE 15.6 iBookstore offers a wide range of books, many for free.

Use the following means to find books:

▶ **Search.** Enter a word from a book name or author name and tap Search on the keyboard to search for it.

- **New & Notable.** A shortlist of New & Notable books appears on the home screen of iBookstore, as shown in Figure 15.6. To see the entire list, tap the arrows, or tap the See All link.

- *New York Times* **bestsellers.** Tap the icon at the bottom of the screen to access the books in the *New York Times* bestseller list (fiction and nonfiction categories).

- **Top Charts.** Top Charts has lists of top paid-for and free books.

- **Purchases.** The Purchases list includes books you've downloaded for free. You can use this list to re-download books you've previously downloaded and then deleted, whether paid for or not.

> TIP: **Stock Up on Free Books Now**
> Stock up iBookshelf with free books early on, so you have something to read when your iPad is out of range of an Internet connection.

Finding Books on a Personal Computer

On a personal computer, you can buy, or download for free, a number of books in ePub format and then transfer them to your iPad via iTunes. The ePub format is an open format that does not contain copy protection, so ePub-formatted files can be freely copied. This is different from iBookstore books, which are copy protected.

Two of the many sites that have ePub-formatted books are as follows:

- **ManyBooks.net.** Includes tons of free books, with recommendations and reviews.

- **iBookstore.com.** This is not Apple's iBookstore, available from iPad, but, rather, an independent web site. It includes free books in ePub format for your iPad, as well as free books and free book readers for your personal computer and cellphones.

To get ePub files into your iTunes library, you must first get the file onto your personal computer. Once you do, just drag and drop the file into iTunes, or select Add to Library from the iTunes application's File menu and locate the file on your computer. The next time you sync to your iPad, the books will be added to your iPad Bookshelf.

Summary

In this lesson, you learned about reading iBooks on your iPad and about how to use the iBookstore and other sources to get free and paid-for books for your iPad. In the next lesson, I describe how to use iTunes to sync multimedia and much more.

LESSON 16

Using iTunes to Sync Multimedia and More

In this lesson, you learn about iTunes and how it works on the iPad as well as personal computers; how to get content for the iPad, including music, movies, and much more; and how to use iTunes to sync your iPad with a personal computer.

Understanding iTunes

iTunes is the funnel for all of Apple's content deals with music producers, Hollywood moguls, book publishers and others, plus access to free content and user-generated content, delivering, syncing, and managing all sorts of items across devices.

As one example of its importance, through iTunes, Apple has been able to enforce a strong, but reasonably user-friendly, digital rights management (DRM) policy for some content, such as movies and some music files. (Some files are DRM-free and can be copied onto any number of devices.) For instance, it may be that no music producer would have ever come up with the idea of having up to five computers authorized to play a piece of music that had only been paid for once—but that's the limit Apple insisted on, and it stuck.

The iTunes interface is a bit odd, not even truly Mac-like in some ways. That's because the original iTunes software was built outside Apple, and then acquired by Apple in a buyout of the company that made it. Apple has improved iTunes over the years, even brought the software onto the iPhone and iPad, but never really overhauled it. iTunes, along with all the content you can access through it, is one of the secrets of the iPad's early success and its continuing usefulness.

Getting Content for the iPad

Typically, the best approach to getting content you want for your iPad is to use the iTunes app on the iPad, rather than the iTunes app on your personal computer. That way, you only have to wait for the download to your iPad to complete before you can use the content. If you get the content on your personal computer first, you have to wait for that download and then wait for it to sync before you see the content on your iPad.

Learning how to use the iTunes app on your iPad also prepares you to operate for longer periods without using a personal computer at all. I believe that, as people get more used to the iPad, it may become the main or only device for some people who couldn't imagine going without a personal computer today.

For now, though, you will still want to sync content downloaded onto your iPad back onto your personal computer. This enables you to delete content from the iPad, knowing you can always get it back relatively quickly by transferring it from your personal computer. You could always download it from iTunes again to your iPad, without cost, but that's a more time-consuming process than syncing with iTunes once the content is already there.

Because it is the best overall approach, this lesson describes how to get content using iTunes on your iPad, and not the iTunes application on your personal computer. It does describe how to sync content from your personal computer to iTunes, so you can use your personal computer as a content store and for content management. If you also prefer to use iTunes on your personal computer to get content, you'll find that what you learn here about using iTunes on your iPad is just about fully applicable to iTunes on a Macintosh or Windows computer as well.

> NOTE: **Getting All Your Content**
> There are some types of content that can't be accessed directly through iPad. This includes content that was purchased or down-

loaded through iTunes before purchasing your iPad, and audio content that you bring into iTunes from CDs. Both scenarios are covered in the section on syncing, which you find later in this lesson. ePad-formatted e-books that you want to use in iBooks, (outlined in Lesson 15, "Using iBooks and the iBookstore") are another type of content that can't be accessed directly through the iPad.

Finding Content

All the major types of content for the iPad—music, movies, TV shows, podcasts, audiobooks, and courseware (iTunes U)—have their own buttons at the bottom of the iTunes screen, as shown in Figure 16.1, and all work in almost exactly the same way.

FIGURE 16.1 The iTunes app is like six stores in one for Music, Movies, TV Shows, Podcasts, Audiobooks, and iTunes U courseware.

Use the buttons at the bottom of the screen to bring up what is basically a separate iTunes Store for each particular category. Then, if you choose Music, Movies, or TV shows, you'll be offered a choice of four buttons on the top, as shown previously for TV Shows in Figure 16.1:

TIP: **Podcasts Come in Audio and Video**
Podcasts can be either audio-only (the original definition) or video podcasts with audio, marked with a video icon. In fact, video podcasts are now so prevalent that it can sometimes seem all too difficult to find a good audio-only podcast.

▶ **Genres.** A genre is a type of content, style, or format similar to the categories you might find in a record or video store. Genres are also used for hits charts and in industry publications and web sites. Use the Genres button for each type of content to see what is available.

▶ **Featured.** This is content that's hot, up and coming, of particular interest, or receiving a lot of promotional support from the publisher or artist. (And yes, there might be money changing hands to help determine what gets featured.) Looking at the Featured list is a good way to keep up with what people are talking about.

▶ **Top Charts.** Charts are not always reliable—for instance, music charts only cover a fraction of what's downloaded on the Internet—but they can be interesting. Use the charts to make sure you aren't missing anything that's broadly popular and that you might like.

▶ **Genius.** The Genius feature works with music files you already have in iTunes to find other content you might like—often reaching across genre boundaries.

Each of these four categories are available for Music, Movies, and TV Shows. Podcasts and Audiobooks don't include the Genius capability. Also, the Genres button is called Categories for these two applications, although it still does basically the same thing. At this writing, using iBooks and the iBookstore lacks both Genius and a Genres/Categories button, so it has only Featured and Top Charts.

The Downloads button takes you to the iPod app and opens the Purchased area; see Lesson 14, "Using iPad for Music and More," for details.

> NOTE: **iBookstore Requires Separate Searches**
> Searching the iTunes store does go across many content types, but it doesn't include books, except for audiobooks. You need to search the iBookstore separately, as described in Lesson 15.

Finding Content in and Across Types

You can find content *within* a type—Music, Movies, TV Shows, Podcasts, Audiobooks, and iTunes U courseware—by pressing the content type button at the bottom. You then look at Genres (or Categories, for Podcasts and Audiobooks, with no similar choice for iTunes U); Featured; Top Charts; or Genius (for Music, Movies, and TV Shows).

You can also find content *across* types —with "hits" in all applicable categories—by using Search. Just enter search terms in the Search area in the upper-right corner and tap Search on the keyboard. Figure 16.2 shows search results for Shakespeare, which is a term that appears in multiple categories.

You can alternate between searching within categories and using the Search function to search across categories. Each type of searching can give you ideas for the other. For instance, your interest in a given musical artist's recordings could also lead to a movie, TV show, or even a course related to that artist or their genre.

When you find an item of interest, tap it to see more information. You can also read reviews, write a review for content you own, or send an email with a link to the item. You can buy, download, or rent the item, depending on what options are available for it. (Remember that rental terms don't begin counting until you start playing the item.)

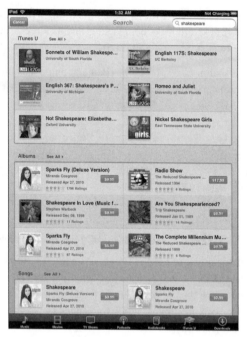

FIGURE 16.2   Shakespeare is a real king of all media.

CAUTION: **Downloads Can Be Slow**

Downloading an item can take a significant amount of time. In testing on a relatively slow broadband connection, it took me a bit less than one-fourth the playing time to download music, and a bit more than one-half the playing time to download video. Check on your own system when downloading so you know just how quickly you can get a music album downloaded before a party, or a video download done before you have friends over for movie night.

Downloading or Purchasing Content

Before buying or downloading music, movies, TV shows, or audiobooks, you need an iTunes Store account. You also need an iTunes Store account to write reviews for any content. To get an iTunes Store account, or to switch among different iTunes Store accounts on your iPad, open the

Settings app and tap Store. You'll then be invited to switch to a different iTunes store account or create a new account.

Purchasing content (or downloading free content) is very similar to downloading an app, as described in Lesson 11, "Getting Apps from the App Store." You tap Install or the price. If the option is offered, tap Buy. For certain videos, you'll have to specify standard definition (480p) or high definition (720p) as well. You'll be asked to sign into your account, if you weren't already, and the item begins downloading. You are given the chance to enter any promotional code you have, such as a gift certificate, before the purchase is final.

New songs and videos are added to the Purchased playlist in the iPod app (see Lesson 14) on your iPad.

You don't need an iTunes Store account to download audio or video podcasts or iTunes U classes. You can listen to or watch the podcast without downloading it, or download it to the iPad and sync it to your iTunes library on your personal computer.

To listen, just press the podcast title. To download, press the Free button and then press Get Episode. New podcasts are added to the Podcast list in iPod (see Lesson 14), where you can listen to or watch them. To get additional episodes in a series, press the Get New Episodes button in the Podcasts list. Video podcasts are also available in the Video app (see Lesson 13, "Playing Videos and YouTube").

Getting ePub Books into iTunes

Getting ePub books into iTunes is perhaps easier to do than it is to explain. It's hard to explain because there are many sources for ePub books; it's easy to do because each step seems quite natural.

You can get an ePub book file as an email attachment or as a file that you download from a web site. Simply save the file in a convenient place, such as your computer desktop.

Open iTunes, and select the Books link in the Library area.

1. Obtain an ePub book file by downloading an email attachment or file that you obtain from a web site to your computer.

2. Open iTunes.

3. To drag and drop the book file into iTunes, open the Books link in the Library area, as shown in Figure 16.3. Drag the ePub file into the Books area.

FIGURE 16.3   You can select a file, or drag and drop it into iTunes.

4. To get the file into iTunes using a dialog, choose File->Add to Library. In the Add to Library dialog box, also shown in Figure 16.3, choose the file you want to upload.

The file is uploaded to the Books area.

5. Sync iTunes to your iPad, as described in the next section.

The book is transferred to your iPad.

Syncing Content with a Personal Computer

When you connect your iPad to your personal computer, iTunes automatically syncs content from iPad to iTunes and vice versa.

When you sync, you are not only transferring new or existing content, you are also able to manage storage on your iPad. Here are the types of content that you can sync with iTunes:

▶ **Media and apps.** Music, movies, TV shows, games and applications from the App Store, music videos, podcasts, and iTunes U collections, audiobooks, books, videos from your computer's movie folder or application, and photos from your computer's photo folder or application.

▶ **Personal information management.** Contacts, calendars, notes, email account settings (from personal computer to iPad only), and web page bookmarks.

Follow these steps to first set options in iTunes on your personal computer, and then synchronize your iPad to it:

1. Connect iPad to your computer.

2. If iTunes doesn't open automatically on your personal computer, open it.

3. In iTunes, select iPad in the sidebar. Tabs for managing syncing to your iPad appear.

4. In the Summary tab, shown in Figure 16.4, set options for managing synchronization.

   Options include setting iPad back to its original settings, which will erase any content on it; syncing only selected songs and videos; and manually managing songs and videos. These options are good to use if your iPad is filling with content.

5. On the Info tab, set options for syncing contacts, calendars, bookmarks, and notes.

FIGURE 16.4   Use iTunes to help manage storage on your iPad.

To sync to Apple's MobileMe, click the Learn More button. Contacts, calendars, mail accounts, and/or notes can all be synced with Outlook on Windows. You can sync contacts only with Google Contacts, Windows Contacts, or Yahoo! Address Book. You can sync bookmarks with Internet Explorer. You can also replace selected information on the iPad on a one time-only basis with information from the personal computer running iTunes.

6. On the Apps tab, set options for syncing apps. You can view your apps and the storage they use, and specify which ones to keep on your iPad; others are stored in iTunes on your personal computer for later use if needed.

7. On the Music tab, set options for syncing music. You can sync all music or only selected playlists, artists, and genres. Unlike apps, you can't manage storage directly, but you can use these estimates to help: 1 minute of music takes up about 1 megabyte, and typical songs are about 3 minutes long, or 3MB in file size.

8. On the Movies tab, set options for syncing movies (TV shows are separate). You can automatically sync all movies or recent ones (by whether they've been watched, or by number of movies), or specify which movies to sync. Specifying individual movies is probably a good idea, as each movie can take up 1GB or more of space.

9. On the TV Shows tab (see Figure 16.5), set options for syncing TV shows. As with movies, you can automatically sync all TV shows or recent ones (by whether they've been watched, or by number of shows), or specify which movies to sync. Specifying individual TV shows is probably a good idea, as a one-hour show can take up half a gigabyte or more of space.

FIGURE 16.5   Managing TV show syncing helps preserve storage on your iPad.

10. In the Podcasts, iTunes U, and Books tabs, set options for sync-ing each type of media content.

Options are similar to other media described in the previous steps, with options to sync all content of a given type, recent items, or specific items. Video podcasts and books that include lots of video clips are likely to be the largest in file size.

11. On the Photos tab, set options for syncing photos and videos.

You can sync all folders or specified ones, and you can include or exclude videos. You can also place videos in folders, and then use the syncing options for those folders to manage storage requirements associated with video.

TIP: **Sync Photos Through iPad**

It's fun to use your iPad as a photo viewer with friends and family, but keep in mind that you can't delete synced photos from the iPad directly, which means you have to manage synced photos via iTunes on your personal computer. It may be helpful to keep a fold-er on your personal computer that is specified for use with your iPad only.

---

12. From any tab where you have changed options, you can click Apply to apply the changes and start a sync. Otherwise, to start a sync using all the new settings, click the Sync button from any tab.

Summary

In this lesson, you learned about iTunes and how it works on the iPad and personal computers; getting content for the iPad, including music and movies; and how to sync iPad with a personal computer.

Now that you've completed the final lesson, you're ready to get the most out of your iPad. Enjoy!

Index

I

R

How can we make this index more useful? Email us at indexes@samspublishing.com

How can we make this index more useful? Email us at indexes@samspublishing.com

W

X-Z

Sams**TeachYourself**
from Sams Publishing

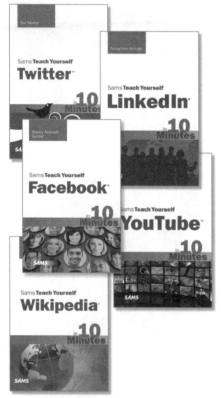

Sams **Teach Yourself in 10 Minutes** offers straightforward, practical answers for fast results.

These small books of 250 pages or less offer tips that point out shortcuts and solutions, cautions that help you avoid common pitfalls, notes that explain additional concepts, and provide additional information. By working through the 10-minute lessons, you learn everything you need to know quickly and easily!

When you only have time for the answers, Sams Teach Yourself books are your best solution.

Visit **informit.com/samsteachyourself** for a complete listing of the products available.